DETOURED

Warrior woman,
Some of God's greatest blessings
are found in detours, just like
the unexpected blessing of
standing on a river bank among
sisters you never knew you had!

God bless you,
And He will!

Jessie Childress

DETOURED

*My Ride Through Cancer
with God as Chauffeur*

TERRIE CHILDRESS

gatekeeper press™
Columbus, Ohio

DETOURED:
My Ride Through Cancer with God as Chauffeur

Published by Gatekeeper Press
2167 Stringtown Rd, Suite 109
Columbus, OH 43123-2989
www.GatekeeperPress.com

Cover design by Angelina Valieva

Library of Congress Control Number: 2020941735

ISBN (paperback): 9781642379655
eISBN: 9781642379662

Printed in the United States of America

CONTENTS

For God—whom without, this book would not have existed. You are the Author of my life, the Co-Author of this book, and the GPS (God of Paths Scouted) through all my life's journeys and detours.

For John—my amazing husband, my rock, my co-warrior, the love of my life, and my greatest gift from God.

For you—the reader, for whom this book was written no matter the path you're on.

FOREWORD
by God

Jesus returned to Jerusalem for one of the Jewish festivals. Inside the city, near the Sheep Gate was the pool of Bethesda with five covered porches. Crowds of sick people—blind, lame, or paralyzed—laid on the porches. One of the men lying there had been sick for thirty-eight years. When Jesus saw him and knew he had been ill for a long time, he asked him, "Do you want to get well?"

"Sir," the invalid replied, "I have no one to help me into the pool when the water is stirred. While I am trying to get in, someone else goes down ahead of me."

Then Jesus said to him, "Rise, take up your mat and walk."

At once the man was cured; he took up his mat and walked.

—John 5:1-9, NIV Streams in the Desert.

PLEASE KNOW, MY child, that sickness and disease are not of Me. They do not come from Me or are ever My desire for you. Though, these trials are opportunities for Me to reach out to you and you to Me, reminding you that I am with you always and here for you to call upon. I will walk the unknown paths alongside you, guiding you through the detours as you grow and strengthen your faith and trust in Me.

I know that sometimes you are more comfortable in your fright, worry and weakness, but I ask of you to take My extended hand and know My love, My care and My restoration. The world makes it so easy to be complacent and weary in your own thoughts as the mind carries you to uncharted places, amplifying your fears rather than your faith.

I see and know your need for healing, and I will provide what you crave. My healing comes not because of who you are, but because of who I am. So, if I asked of you what I asked of the lame man, "Do you want to get well?" would you have the fortitude to roll up your mat and walk? My child, it is easier to move the wheels of a cart that is already in motion than one that is sitting idle.

Wherever you trod, I am already there.

I tell you, blessed one, pack lightly through life's journeys and rigid terrains. Take only what you need and leave the rest, filling your knapsack especially and completely with faith and reliance in Me. I will carry the remainder of what is necessary for your travels. And I will carry you.

Do not be anxious about anything,
   but in everything, by prayer and petition,
   with thanksgiving, present your requests to God.

   —Philippians 4:6, NIV Streams in the Desert.

What do you want Me to do for you?

   —Matthew 20:32, NIV Streams in the Desert.

INTRODUCTION

JUNE 2015. THAT was the month and year I'd planned to retire from the educational arena. But I've heard it said, 'If you want to hear God laugh, tell Him your plans.' The plans we make for ourselves and God's plans for us are rarely in alignment.

I had worked in education as a secretary, a classroom teacher, and an instructional reading assistant for twenty-four years, and I wanted to do something different. I wanted to get back to my writing desk. I had written eleven manuscripts for children's books in the past few years, having one of them published in 2011. I was also entertaining the idea of becoming a freelance editor and writing coach. I'd recently been hired as a part-time writing coach by one of my colleagues needing assistance on a thesis, and later, a dissertation.

My plans were falling into place and coming together quite nicely. I thought. But, like anyone, I didn't factor in the possibility of a diversion from my agenda. My plans were simple, after all, on an expressway in which I had great familiarity and one that I could coast with my eyes wide closed. I just didn't expect to be blindsided out of nowhere like running a *Stop* sign hidden by brush. Or a cancer camouflaged by cysts.

We never sketch out a 'Plan B,' because we are the inventors of and the ones in control of 'Plan A.' Right? Wrong. God is in control of every plan and turn in our lives. But, with us exempting Him from our outline, we like to think and truly believe that we are the sole hands holding the reigns that execute the plan; hence, 'Plan B' often not being part of our original design.

None of us know what we have up ahead. But God knows. And through our regular paths and daily routines, He prepares and secures us for the road—all the roads—forward.

"*Accept yourself in your weariness, knowing that I understand how difficult your journey has been. I have gifted you with fragility, providing opportunities for your spirit to blossom in My Presence. Accept this gift as a sacred treasure: delicate yet glowing with brilliant Light. Rather than struggling to disguise or deny your weakness, allow Me to bless you richly through it.*"—Isaiah 42:3; Isaiah 54:10; Romans 8:26. Sarah Young, *Jesus Calling*, (Nashville: Thomas Nelson, 2004), 235.

It is my sincere belief and experience in writing this title that God is the Co-Author, if not the lone Author, of the pages following, as He scrolled the words of each chapter through my mind both at and away from the keyboard. Though, a dear friend remarked that God used me as the vessel for the story. And that was my honor.

So, this is the book that God and I have written…for you.

1ˢᵀ STOP *Driving Lessons (Apply Within)*

THEY SAY, 'TIME flies,' and I believe it does. But not this year.

Maybe it was because we had a new school principal or a whole new block master schedule, or both. Whatever the case, it was the most grueling, hard, and demanding year that I'd ever experienced in my career.

I was the fourth and fifth grade reading instructional assistant, and my body and mind was in constant overdrive. I had to run (literally) on a full tank everyday with few stops or even yields in my path. The school was a pod school which meant going outside to leave one grade level building to enter another. It also meant having to look the weather's elements right in the face—from the bitter cold, to the pouring rain, to the unbelievably windy, to the warm sun that sprinkled allergies in its wake.

My schedule was particularly hectic, moving myself and my teaching materials from one building to another as fast as I could travel. I felt like I had a stoplight hanging above me that only blinked green. I would wait and hope for a cautioned yellow light to appear from time to time, but it never showed itself. It was just as well. I would have kept running through it, anyway.

I loved the kids, every one of them, as well as the companion teachers I joined and assisted in the classrooms. But they were stressed, too—the teachers and the kids—from this new master schedule that doubled all our workloads.

This new block timetable put us on an eight-day rotation cycle, and every day stowed a different schedule than the day before it. I had to study and memorize my plan book at the beginning of every morning, reviewing where I was to be when, for how long, and what my lesson plans were for that day between both grade levels I served.

Even though this new schedule began in the middle of October and went through the end of the school year, I never could routinely remember the schedule of each day, mainly because there was no routine to it. Each new day had a designated number up through Day 8. After Day 8, we would start all over again with Day 1.

The new schedule also left the kids and faculty with little or no time for rest, play, or planning. And, if the hands of time within the bright clock's face were ever positioned looking out the window toward the playground chiming a break, the schedule had little space or patience for outdoor recess, causing the clock's hands to refrain and continue spinning in utter silence among the other working hands in the room.

Because the blocks of time inside every classroom had grown from minutes to hours at a time, I knew that I would be asked to expand my capacity from assisting to co-teaching. And, that's exactly what happened, as the teachers split the classes into two, and sometimes three, groups. With a degree in Paraprofessional Elementary Education, I was happy and experienced enough to take on this broadened role. And I enjoyed it. For the first two weeks. Then, my excitement became obscured beneath the scope of complete exhaustion when the schedule and labor collided, draining me in every facet, physically and mentally.

The only days I started looking forward to were Saturdays

and Sundays. But when the clock struck 3:00 p.m. on Saturday afternoon, I felt the weekend slipping away and Monday morning already tapping me on the back, gesturing me to turn around and catch a glimpse of its approaching debut, waiting and peering from behind the peaceful curtains of my weekend rest.

I knew this wasn't right. God doesn't want us to just enjoy and bask in two days a week. He wants us to appreciate every day, every hour, and every moment.

When Monday morning reared its ugly head, the teachers and students alike came in disheveled and worn out like we'd had no weekend at all. The kids would have reading block to start off their week. And, the next day, math would fall into that time slot. Or they would go to specials like music, art, or library. Reading would be forty-five minutes one day and ninety minutes the next. And some days, math and reading were coupled into a three-hour time frame without students being provided any time for recreational movement at all.

But that became short-lived when the teachers began incorporating movement opportunities for students inside of the lesson plans and learning sessions. How ingenious! This method of teaching provided a more engaging and memorable learning experience for the kids, which was the first and only blessing that this new master schedule lent! It refueled the students' brains and recharged their bodies. Of course, the teachers did their part during these movement lessons as we all danced, did jumping jacks, and clapped, stomped—clapped, clapped, stomped—along.

My life at school was invariantly busy, my lunch period late and short, regardless of the designated day. And I walked faster and harder than I ever imagined I could, every day. It was like God was grooming me for something.

You've heard the quote, 'Everything happens for a reason.'

That line replayed itself a lot in my head, and I knew that God had a purpose for continuing to keep me on this nonstop merry-go-round that held the rag doll of me on its floor at the end of each day. I just couldn't imagine what purpose my running around like I was in training for a marathon all day would be. But I would soon find out.

2ND STOP *Flashing Lights*

MARCH 17, 2014. I had asked for this day off to watch the annual St. Patrick's Day celebration event on QVC. I watched it every year, and while I considered specifying the day's leave from work as a *sick* day, which could have been earmarked simply, Mental Health Day Needed, thus, coinciding with the year I was having, I shooed that thought away and kept it as a *personal* day request.

As I was filling out the leave form, my imagination was still trying to influence my indicated day choice by feeding me a story that played out as my having an appointment with my breast specialist in Charlottesville. But I shooed that bad thought away, too.

The truth was I hadn't scheduled a mammogram or seen my breast specialist for two years. I don't know how I had let that time pass when I'd always been so faithful on making that appointment.

My breasts were very dense, leaving most mammograms and specialist visits in the dark as to what were cysts and what could be something else. I'd had a mammogram every year since the age of twenty-five when a suspicious cyst disguised itself as a 99.9% certain cancer diagnosis. I breathed a sigh of relief when the results came back showing only a cyst. Though, this event began the cycle of my needing to have yearly, and sometimes biyearly, mammograms to maintain a vigil watch.

Throughout my course of mammograms each year, I was told on only two occasions, "We'll see you in a year."

The other visits were always followed up with an ultrasound, an MRI, and another ultrasound to clarify the findings on the MRI. I often wondered, *Is that too much radiation in one year? One week? One day?*

The night preceding my St. Patrick's *personal* day, a good amount of snow was forecasted to fall through the overnight. As luck would have it, schools across the region were closed the next morning beneath a beautiful March snowfall. So, I didn't have to use a *personal* day after all. It was now a *snow* day!

QVC's St. Patrick's Day celebration is the one day that I shop most with them, because they have special guests from Ireland who come to sell their products with a story behind each creation. I also enjoy listening to the Irish dialect as the guests share their heritage and traditions. Since I've never visited Ireland, I feel like every year on March 17th watching QVC, that in some small way, I did get to visit at the day's end.

Sometimes, I will preview the upcoming Irish items online and order one or two things ahead of time for fear of them selling out quickly if I would otherwise wait.

This year, I had spotted an Irish fairy pendant necklace hanging among the 'sneak peek' items. She was stunning and quite detailed, crafted three-dimensionally like a figurine done in sterling silver. Facing frontward, she had a full bodice with a face, bust, sculpted outfit, and the sweetest pointed toes. A small shamrock with light green stones dangled from her hand, and she was adorned with two marquise-shaped emerald stone wings framing her back.

I was so excited to receive this pendant a week before the big show. And, when I opened her box, I gasped, taking her out and wrapping her around my neck. I don't know exactly how to describe it, but I do know that as soon as my hands dropped from hooking the chain, I was overwhelmed by an instant calming peace. So, this piece brought me peace. And a little bit more.

I, of course, had my Irish fairy necklace garnished around my neck on St. Patrick's Day. And, when she was presented on-air, she was described by her Irish creator as, "a guardian angel that makes sure you're always okay." I thought that was a perfect description of her.

Later that afternoon as I walked through the kitchen, I was rubbing my hand across my fairy pendant. Out of nowhere, I felt this nudge, accompanied by a powerful urge, for me to go pick up the phone and schedule a real appointment with my breast specialist. I ignored the nudge and passed by the phone, only to circle around and be redirected back toward it.

My thoughts were almost as speechless as my tongue. *What's going on? Where did this come from? Why do I need to call today? I'm missing my show!* As I contemplated all of this, I continued rubbing my hand over the fairy 'angel,' making no connection to her in this unexplainable dilemma I was in.

The business card for Dr. Salydar, my breast specialist, was in the cabinet just above the phone. I stood there for only a second before my hand opened the door and reached in for the card. I grabbed the phone and sat down to punch in the number, completely uncertain of how I got here and why I was even doing this.

When Dr. Salydar's nurse answered the phone and I told her my name, she remembered me and was very kind. However, she was unsure if I could be seen anytime soon by

Dr. Salydar, because as I mentioned earlier, I had not followed up with her for two years. The nurse indicated that she would speak with the doctor and get back to me.

Hours later, I received a call back from Nurse Pam with a scheduled mammogram and appointment to see Dr. Salydar, both on the same day: Wednesday, April 16, 2014.

When I hung up, I was glad I'd made the appointment. I had been experiencing some unusual pain in my right breast lately. I didn't think anything of it, as cysts are painful. But I think my Irish 'angel' suspected a little something more. And, I truly believe that hers were the wings that carried me toward the phone that day as I held onto her.

God's angels come in all shapes, sizes, and forms. Mine just happened to come from a little corner of Ireland.

3RD STOP *Divided Highway*

WE ALL KNOW the cliché, 'No pain. No gain.' And, while I've never really been a fan of that saying—perhaps because it's spoken so often—it does speak truth. And, maybe that's why it *is* spoken so often.

"Every difficult task that comes across your path—every one that you would rather not do, that will take the most effort, cause the most pain and be the greatest struggle—brings a blessing with it. And refusing to do it regardless of the personal cost is to miss the blessing. Every difficult stretch of road on which you see the Master's footprints and along which He calls you to follow Him leads unquestionably to blessings. And they are blessings you will never receive unless you travel the steep and thorny path." —J.R. Miller, NIV Streams in the Desert.

So, with that, there's a whole new perspective on 'No pain. No gain.' More importantly, there's a new profound definition and purpose behind that infamous saying. And maybe, that's why it has stuck.

Just two days before my phone call to Dr. Salydar, I had experienced excruciating pain on the outer side of my right breast. I'd had this pain before. And each time, it concerned me more because it was so unbearable, even debilitating.

This pain would immediately take my breath away, cause me to perspire, and eventually double me over in a sitting position where I would begin to massage and apply pressure to the pain's location for roughly five to ten minutes before I could re-compose, and the pain dissipate. Even though this pain was like that of no other I'd had in my breasts before, I knew that it was what it always was...a cyst. But I also knew that this cyst had to be a sizable one to impose that amount of pain. And, every time I encountered this pain, I wondered what would happen if it wouldn't let up the next time.

Because these episodes were sporadic, I battled some of them at school, which led me to excuse myself to the bathroom frequently. But, the one that happened two days before St. Patrick's Day unfolded in the back seat of our friends' car on the way back from a daytrip to Shenandoah National Park. I was already tired from our day of riding and walking, so I didn't really have the strength for this episode. Ironically, it was the one that I ended up needing to be the strongest for. As my husband conversed up front in the passenger's seat beside Jim, I became speechless and motionless in the back seat beside Sharon. Fortunately, Sharon was on her phone, missing my instantly moistened face and rapid breathing as I looked out the side window and endured a pain that felt humanly oppressive to the conscious. And, just like with any pain after it finally leaves your body and time passes, you tend to forget that you were ever in it. Until it comes back again.

"Breast cancer is a painless cancer. So, if your breasts hurt or you experience pain in one, or both, of them, that's a sure sign that it's a cyst."

Those are the words that had been declared to me over the years by doctors and radiologists alike. But what I had been told for so long by these professionals was becoming allegory in these changing times. And my blessing, disguised as pain (God's science), was about to debunk earthly science and prove it horribly wrong.

4TH STOP *New Traffic Pattern Ahead*

M Y MAMMOGRAM WAS early the morning of April 16, 2014. I wasn't nervous. It was routine as usual. As a matter of fact, I had the routine down quite well as a mammography veteran of twenty-two years at the age of forty-nine.

First, the mammogram would take place; second, would be my appointment with Dr. Salydar at her office down the hall where she would examine me and discuss the question marks of my mammogram. Third, I'd be off to the ultrasound room where Dr. Salydar would prepare to venture through the thick, foggy forests that were my breasts in search of the hidden answers. The answers were routinely discovered in the shape of a cyst, masked by density and surrounded by a haze of massive white webbing that even Charlotte the spider wouldn't have wanted to tread upon. For her demise in the book *Charlotte's Web* would have come much sooner, for sure.

Waiting with John on the third floor of Martha Jefferson's Outpatient Center, my name was called quickly. *A benefit of being an early bird,* I thought. *That's a good perk, and, incentive to schedule early in the morning.*

My mammogram pictures were snapping along, providing their usual amount of painful flashes when the photographer tech, staring hard at her computer screen, said, "If Dr. Salydar wants me to take more pictures of you later, tell her I'll be glad to do that."

"Okay," I said. "I'll let her know."

But, that's not what I wanted to say. I wanted to say what I was thinking. *What does that mean? Are you seeing something? Dr. Salydar has never asked for more pictures. Why do you think she would want more pictures?*

My appointment with Dr. Salydar was scheduled beyond two hours of the mammography appointment, so John and I decided to go grab some breakfast at the Tip Top Restaurant.

Over breakfast, I told John what the tech had said. "Something's up," I commented. "The techs have never said that to me before, so I'm a bit puzzled."

"Maybe the tech is new and just isn't sure if she took enough pictures," John replied.

"My breasts would debate that," I shot back. They had posed every which way for her as she positioned them beneath the glass plate. "And, I can't remember having so many pictures and different angles taken of my breasts before," I continued.

The worry fell from me, or was taken from me, at that moment as a calm reassurance settled in. *I haven't seen this tech before, although it's been two years since I've been here. But maybe she is new and just wants to make sure that Dr. Salydar has good, clear pictures. Maybe they weren't that clear and that's why she offered retakes,* I rationalized. That had to be it.

Dr. Salydar was as sweet as she always was when she entered the exam room. She was also as professional and thorough as always, and I knew I was in good hands every time I saw her. She was passionate and serious about her work as a breast specialist, and she wasted no time jumping right in to ask me if I'd had any problems or unusual discomfort in my breasts. I immediately told her of the painful episodes I had been experiencing in my right breast.

"The mammogram showed something in your right breast, and I have your pictures hanging right outside the door. Follow me," Dr. Salydar said.

As I studied the pictures, she navigated me through, pointing to what appeared to look like a pool of cysts. Multiple cysts. That was a new snapshot from routine for me, as the past photos had always shown one lone cyst.

"Do you think they're cysts?" I asked her.

"I don't know. That's what we're going to find out," Dr. Salydar replied.

While her thoroughness and determination to solve every mystery of the breast are the main things I love about Dr. Salydar, *that* response from her was a new answer than what she had said to me in earlier visits of my prior years with her.

I was sent to Dr. Salydar by my primary care physician years ago when he found something in my left breast during an annual physical. And, there was another new— today, for the first time, it was my right breast in question. For twenty-two years my left breast was the one that had been watched time and again with great suspicion, always containing an unidentified object. And that object was later found to be a single cyst which had, in time, grown into the size of a golf ball. Tee time, anyone? I bet that cyst would have made a hole in one on the greens at first strike!

In the ultrasound room, Dr. Salydar struggled to obtain a clear view as she explored around the outside perimeter of my right breast. I watched as she came upon what looked to be five cysts standing side by side like they were about to perform in a dancing kick line.

"I'm going to send you back over to mammography to get some more pictures. Spot images," Dr. Salydar remarked.

And there it was. The opportunity for me to deliver this morning's message to Dr. Salydar from the mammography tech.

"The tech told me this morning that if you wanted more pictures, she'd be glad to take them for you," I delivered.

"That's great," replied Dr. Salydar. "Just stay in your robe, and I'll send you back down to them wearing that so you don't have to change out again," she commented as I followed her out of the ultrasound room.

Dr. Salydar approached her nurse and asked that she contact mammography to let them know I was returning now. I, in turn, asked if Dr. Salydar's staff would inform John so he would know where I was going and wouldn't worry. What a crazy blend of words. Of course, he would worry. As I did. When the nurse opened the door to John's waiting area, she kindly invited him to walk with her and me back to mammography screening.

As the nurse guided John and me toward a back door that led to the mammogram hallway, Dr. Salydar yelled to her nurse from behind, "And I want an MRI on Terrie, no matter what!"

Here I was on my way to 'spot imaging'—a second mammogram just hours from my first one. That was another new from my usual routine visit. And, the panic in Dr. Salydar's voice hollering for a breast MRI on me was alarmingly new.

John and I got separated as he was shown to a waiting room, while I was taken on to a Patient Waiting Hall with a couch. It was an empty couch in an emptier hall with not one soul around and no distractions to help ward off the menagerie of terrifying thoughts and scenarios that penetrated the walls of my mind. I imagined all kinds of things. But what I was conjecturing was not what bothered me as much as what

I was feeling. It was like a passing thought, and even a soft sound, whispering to me and letting me know in the most subtle way it could, that this time, everything was going to be new. The routine was over.

5TH STOP *Rough Road Ahead*

WHEN I RETURNED to Dr. Salydar's office, my right breast was sore and aching. I thought *I* was surprised to be returning to mammography, but it turned out my brain didn't get the message to my right breast until it found itself pressed and motionless, once again, beneath the crushing glass. It was flipped this way and that like a stuffed elephant. And the pain from each filming felt elephant sized.

After I redressed and appeared at Dr. Salydar's office check-out window, an MRI appointment was waiting for me, scheduled for 7:30 a.m. on Tuesday, April 22nd. But I don't think Dr. Salydar wanted to wait that long. I had earlier overheard her ask for it today, and then question in disgust, "What do you mean you only do breast MRI's in the early mornings?"

So, I knew she had snatched the earliest, but unsuitably, available appointment. And I could sense her swelling anxiousness in that phone call. Anxiety had a lot of friends today.

Dr. Salydar had been trying to reach me on my cell phone since the afternoon of my MRI, but my phone was turned off, as I was at home. So, I didn't receive her panicked message until the afternoon of the next day when I turned on my phone to call John as I was leaving school. But John called

17

me first, intercepting my listening of Dr. Salydar's message, to inform me that Nurse Pam had called the home phone and was frantically trying to reach me before the close of day. John didn't know why, as the nurse's voice just begged my return call. This urgency all around me, all at once, jolted me and forced me into a reality that was anything but real.

I quickly hung up with John and listened to now, three messages awaiting me on my phone—one from Dr. Salydar and two from Nurse Pam—all echoing the same announcement that "something showed on the MRI, and you need to come in right away for another ultrasound and a possible needle biopsy."

I pulled off the road and parked in a vacant lot so I could call the nurse and give my full attention to this startling information. I wanted to be sitting still with my mind unoccupied and undistracted by other moving objects around me. And I had to be able to write down my appointment time. Funny thing was that after hearing Nurse Pam now speaking into my ear about a needle biopsy, I struggled to process things, let alone write. I forget how many times I confirmed my appointment with her, which was scheduled for tomorrow at two o'clock. It was hard to stamp it into my brain following the words, 'needle biopsy.'

But Nurse Pam had been in the arena of patience (patients) walking this rope before, so she held on and repeated things with a gentle, understanding and reassuring tone until she knew I had secured the received information on the other end of the phone (rope).

After the nurse and I hung up, I called John, still sitting parked in my car. I couldn't tell him my conversation with Nurse Pam over the phone, and I wouldn't let myself say the words. So, I just told him that I had reached the nurse and had an appointment for tomorrow afternoon, and I'd talk with him more when I got home. (Thank the Lord for the napkin lying in front of me on the car's console; for without that, I probably would've forgotten my appointment time of two o'clock tomorrow, again. And ever since that day, I keep a napkin laying up front in my car just for writing purposes.)

John was first taken aback by the news of my needing a needle biopsy. But his surprise was quickly replaced by gratefulness as he held me and reminded (us both) of Dr. Salydar's consistent thoroughness. My heart slowed in its pounding, as I followed suit of John's always reasoning words.

My last appointment with Dr. Salydar, just a week and one day ago, ended with us hugging at the exit door. And today, April 24th, we were embracing again at the entrance door as she greeted John and me.

I wanted and needed John by my side, and he wanted to be there, so Dr. Salydar led us both back to the ultrasound room. As she got the ultrasound machine set up, she was telling us that the MRI had shown something in my right breast that hadn't appeared on the mammogram, or, on the ultrasound. She said also that she had been informed just hours after my MRI that something new had surfaced—something hiding behind some cysts—and, when a shadowed area became more pronounced from the dye that was injected intravenously into me, the shadowy image came more clearly into focus as it was exposed in its hiding place. Dr. Salydar's goal was to find it now on the ultrasound so she could obtain a clear point of entrance to biopsy it.

John and I both viewed the screen with Dr. Salydar, our eyes following her every move through the fog and dance line of the five cysts still standing there since last week's ultrasound. And then, there it was—peeking out from behind the second cyst line dancer—a small black mass casting its shadow above the heads of all others. Now, completely stealing the show!

As Dr. Salydar zoomed in closer, Nurse Pam entered the room, almost on cue, and began prepping me and preparing the tools for Dr. Salydar to proceed with the needle biopsy. I was repositioned with my back now turned away from Dr. Salydar and the screen. She used the ultrasound's monitor as her guide inward. I held on tight to the nurse's hand, as the needle's initial entry into my right breast caused me to wince in excruciating, unexpected pain that seemed to steal every breath of air inside of me. Dr. Salydar announced that I would feel no more pain as that throughout the rest of the procedure. And I didn't, as I laid there thinking, *how could I feel further pain with no breath?*

John, like the doctor he should have been, watched the entire televised biopsy, as Dr. Salydar took several samples. When she prepared to exit my right breast, she told me I would feel and hear a brief rubber band-like snap. I was glad that the clapping sound of the rubber band was greater than its predictable pain. I was numb to its threat so remained unharmed in its force. Nurse Pam quickly began sewing and bandaging me up.

As I laid there being mended back together, I commented to Dr. Salydar, "I don't mean for this to sound radical, because I'm not someone who thinks on the extreme, but if this comes back benign, should I consider a bilateral mastectomy just because my breasts constantly stock and replay mysteries?"

"I don't think that sounds radical at all," Dr. Salydar replied. "But, I'm pretty sure this is cancer. I don't expect it to come back benign."

At this point, she was holding my hand and telling me with her eyes what she had just said with her mouth. My mind immediately recalled the two years I'd missed scheduling mammograms and visits with her.

My lips quivered, causing my words to shake as they

fell from the rim. "The two years I missed having my mammograms and follow-ups with you, will that time lost cause the pendulum on this diagnosis to swing toward a more severe case or stage?" I grimaced at the thought of my negligence in this surrealness.

"No, not at all. I think it's been caught as early as it could be, and it may not have shown before now," Dr. Salydar stated, confidently.

As Dr. Salydar got ready to leave, she leaned over and hugged me, saying that she'd call me to let me know for certain at the top of next week. Today was Thursday, and I was, in an odd way, thankful for the 'heads up' of the practically undeniable diagnosis. So, I thought I could wait for five more days. Or, I hoped I could. It was a gift of time to let the possibility saturate through me.

When the nurse finished bandaging me, she hugged me, and then sat down beside me. "Listen," she began. "This is just a bump in the road. That's all it is. Dr. Salydar will take care of this, and you'll get back to your life. It's just a bump in the road."

As John and I walked down the hall from the office, he stretched his arm across my shoulder, and tears welled up from the inside out of me.

"Everything's going to be okay, sweetie," he said. "We're going to get through this together, so don't worry."

"I know, honey," I replied.

But I didn't believe my own words. And at this moment, I couldn't even stir up belief in his words. I knew that we'd get through all this together; I just didn't know how 'okay' it was all going to be. I knew that God was going to carry John and me through this. But I couldn't even grasp the real understanding of that yet, because I'd never been at this place in my life before where I was about to find out what God was, who He *really* was, and what He was truly capable of.

A lot of thoughts consumed my mind on the quiet ride home. *Twenty-two years of mammograms and ultrasounds with a few MRI's sprinkled in. How did this happen?* I asked myself while scolding myself at the same time for the two years I'd missed. I had been so diligent, so proactive in being screened and checked every year since the age of twenty-five, . . . minus two. *That should count for something, shouldn't it?* And then the famous quote by Jean de La Fontaine jarred me as it scrolled across my mind, "A person often meets his destiny on the road he took to avoid it."

To slow my racing mind, I thought back to the nurse's comment about 'a bump in the road.' I pondered the idea that some people see 'a bump in the road' as a hindrance when maybe, it's really a *Slow Down* sign for us to smell the flowers and count our blessings. I didn't believe in the latter part today. *This* bump in *my* road was a hindrance—a boomerang that struck me at the very core of my life and my existence in it. And, it wasn't a *Slow Down* sign. It was a sign with bright red flashing lights that halted my whole being with its eminent warning, *Prepare to Stop.*

6TH STOP *Caution*

W HEN JOHN AND I arrived home from hearing the diagnosis of my possible breast cancer, we talked about the family and friends we wanted to call. The list was short because Mom's birthday was Sunday, April 27th, and I didn't want to spoil that. My mom loves her birthday and embraces it more than anyone I've ever known.

I saw a small wooden sign in a primitive shop once that had the words inscribed, *"Don't dread getting old. It's a privilege denied to many."*—Unknown.

I think Mom is the epitome of that. She has never dreaded her birthday. She celebrates a new year of life every year, even most times, making her own dinner reservations with the family (instead of vice versa) at a place she's sure will sing 'Happy Birthday' to her with a lit candle glowing atop a tasty dessert.

John and I sat on the couch deciding whom we would tell, still absorbing the news of probability ourselves with both our stomachs empty and only our minds churning.

My sister, Vickie, was the first I named to call. I had to tell Vickie because she was not only my sister, she was my best friend. We were going to be meeting in Winchester on Saturday to celebrate Mom's birthday a day early, and Vickie would be able to see right through me that something was off, and I couldn't tell her there around Mom.

Wanting to tell Vickie was ironic for two reasons, though. She's always said that she 'doesn't like crises,' and, she doesn't like to keep secrets from Mom that she believes she should know. But I wanted and needed to share this with Vickie, and I knew that something of this magnitude, she would want to know and would, respectfully, keep it quiet from Mom so as not to upset her birthday.

When I picked up the phone to dial Vickie's number, I had no idea what I was going to say or if my tears would allow words to be spoken at all. So, I did what anyone would do who had a calm, soft-spoken, level-headed, compassionate husband. I handed the phone to John.

After they exchanged some general conversation, John proceeded to tell Vickie. And, he cautioned her that it was still just a chance, though John and I were preparing ourselves for the absolute as we awaited Dr. Salydar's confirmation call in the days ahead.

Once John handed me the phone, my being able now to talk since the difficult data had been communicated, Vickie and I engaged in an extraordinary conversation that was paralleled in both of us wanting to comfort the other. It was a colloquy of tears, humor, reassurance, and faith. Vickie agreed to keep this secret from Mom, and in fact, believed that regardless of Mom having an upcoming birthday, that she didn't need to know anything until we received a definitive word from Dr. Salydar. I bet that's why God made Vickie the older sister—she can think on her feet, and her wisdom precedes her.

When we hung up, I felt closer to Vickie than ever, and I knew our relationship was going to grow even stronger no matter what the diagnosis because we were sisters, best friends, and now, confidants with a mission! (Vickie didn't know it yet, but she was going to play an instrumental part with a key role in the weeks to come that she would never have believed she could do. But I knew she could. Vickie and I would both discover that we were stronger than we thought we were.)

The only other people that John and I decided to tell that evening were our good friends, Jim and Sharon, and John's family.

I do think we ate supper at some point that night, but I don't remember when or what. And, I'm not sure John remembers eating at all.

This is what I do remember. I was, and am, so grateful to have the blessing of John as my husband and the honor to be his wife. And I knew, without a doubt, that whatever lay ahead for us, that we were going to hold up and stand by each other. It's just always been that way with John and me.

Some people say that marriage is hard work. But I believe that it's teamwork, compromise, and unconditional love. John and I almost always fall into the same peg hole on everything. And, at times, when we don't make it to the same hole at the same time, our pegs eventually end up meeting there. God has always met us at that opening, because marriage doesn't just take two; it takes three—God at the helm, and John and I always following where He navigates.

So, "in sickness and in health," John and I prepared to plunge in and hold on to each other for an impending ride into depths we knew no bottom, with twists and unseen turns, and the unknown of where it would take us, and where it would drop us off.

I can't recall all the images that swam through my mind as my head finally hit the pillow that night. I laid there thinking back to the biopsy, remembering the pain at the onset of the procedure, which felt and seemed like more than the work of a needle. I thought about the likely outcome from the biopsy and the soreness I felt from it now.

As I stared up at the ceiling, it became arduous to keep any panic that was trying to swell up inside me at bay. So, I told myself, "You might not even have cancer. Your breasts have fooled doctors, countless times before. This cancer is just another possibility, not a reality."

That was my bedtime story.

7TH STOP *Yield*

WE'VE ALL DONE it. Wished for something through thought or spoken word that we didn't really want, but joked about, almost making ourselves believe that we could want it. These wishes are usually followed by the aphorism, 'Be careful what you wish for.' I don't think truer words have ever been spoken, because on many occasions, their warning comes to certain fruition.

I did that. I made wishful remarks, horrible statements, and had unbelievable words cross my lips about the one thing on my body (okay, two things) that I saw as eyesores that were always in my way. And even clothed, they made the rest of me look bigger. Though, my John always told me that I bought my clothes too big, giving off a false image of myself when I looked in the mirror.

My breasts used to be a small 34B. Ideal little molehills. But when I hit my early-to-mid forties, it was truly amazing the mountainous ranges that appeared before my eyes, practically overnight. My new size . . . 40D!

I was 5'8" and 160 pounds, so the proportion of these ridges was, I thought, quite noticeable. They always seemed to enter a room before the rest of me arrived. Whenever QVC is selling a particular brand handbag, the guest often says, "Lead with the handbag."

Do you know how big that bag would have to be to lead ahead of me? I would internally reply.

So now, in full disclosure, because we're all family in the Lord and perfectly imperfect humans, I must confess my wishful remarks and thoroughly embarrassing declarations about myself to you. Only three people before you know these—John, Mom, and Vickie. I decided to share these with you because I want you to believe what I used to not in myself. You are beautiful and molded by God just the way you should be, from the inside out. Your landscape is an original, so you can never be replaced even if you wish to be redone. Your beauty is yours alone because God wants to show you off as His creation, His masterpiece that He only made a one-of-a-kind of . . . YOU.

The statements I made about my breasts were shameful, and I was often uttering this one to my mom: "I wish I could just have the dumb things cut off and donated to science. I would probably be a millionaire with as much as I have, not to mention the scientific findings that may come from them."

"Terrie, don't say that!" Mom would shoot back. "There are lots of women who would love to have what you have."

"Well, I'm sure I have enough to share with all of them," I thoughtlessly retorted.

And then, in late March 2014 when I received my navy merino wool, made in Ireland, zip sweater from QVC's St. Patrick's Day celebration, I stood in front of our hallway mirror and said, "This sweater would look great on me if it weren't for my breasts. I'll keep it, though, because if I order the next size up, it will hang on me. Maybe, I just won't zip it."

John, overhearing me, commented, "Sweetie, it looks great on you now. It fits you perfectly. You need to wear it. Zipped or unzipped, you don't have any sweater like that, and you look good in navy."

My husband is the most beautiful man I've ever known besides my father, because he's so loving and always knows what to say to me. And, I know he means it. (I do wonder sometimes, though, if he might need to update his eyeglass prescription.)

But, the absolute most unthinkable thing I've ever said spilled out of my mouth, without a thought, following an unbelievable day at work.

The kids were, well, kids. But today their anxious behavior and antics were escalated because of an inappropriate comment made to them by another campus teacher. And there was absolutely nothing I could do about it except pat it down with the kids when I had a moment of opportunity alone with them. The students quickly revisited the matter with me, and I said to them, "Guys, don't even let that stay stored in your head for a second. Delete it like you delete junk on your computer. Trust me. Just let it roll by and off you, because you're better than that, and you know it."

As I watched some of their fingers raise to tap the air of an imaginary 'delete' key, I was hopeful that would delete it from my storage compartment as well. But it didn't. My job was crazy enough this year without having to be witness to words that the kids should never have been within earshot of spat out so quickly and thoughtlessly toward them. I had held this circumstance inside of me all day to share only with John later.

When I got home, before I had even told John what happened, I decided to begin with a descriptive comparison of which my mind had no measure. Standing at the kitchen sink trying to scrub the day off my hands, my thoughts floating inside of a wafting soap bubble imagining nothing worse than this job, I blurted out to John, "I'd rather have cancer. Since this job is like cancer, what would the difference be?"

I knew nothing of cancer except the loved ones it'd taken from me. That should have been enough for me to never have voiced those words. I knew better than to tempt, or carelessly wish, for such a destructive and deadly disease. I had never experienced it myself within my own body, and I certainly didn't ever want to.

I reflected on the gravity of my comment throughout the duration of that evening. And I was so ashamed, mostly of my blatant selfishness and lack of thought for those currently afflicted by cancer who would trade me places every day, any day.

I had apologized to John, and he, gently embracing me, accepted my plea. I hoped that God would also accept my apology for such a despicable statement, and I knew that He would. But still the remnants of that horrid remark shook my soul and pierced my thoughts. *I can't believe I said that. Does God know I didn't mean it? Lord, please forgive me. What in the world is wrong with me to say such a thing? For I know not how blessed I am.*

And when I thought back to my ghastly proclamation a few months later, I was completely paralyzed by the actuality of my own words. I thought, *Quite obviously, God heard me speak those.* But what I didn't know was that His full awareness of me was what He was going to use to prepare me, and bless me, for what was to come.

8ᵀᴴ STOP Detour

TODAY, TUESDAY, APRIL 29ᵗʰ' was the day that I was to receive the confirmation phone call from Dr. Salydar conveying whether her suspicions of my having breast cancer were correct. I had spoken to her office late last evening and was told that my reports had just come in and that Dr. Salydar would be calling me with the results in the morning. *This* morning.

I was working with a fifth-grade student on a writing assignment when the phone in my pocket broke out into a soft, but daunting, song. As I reached in and viewed the phone number on the screen, Dr. Salydar was the music on the other end. The classroom teacher knew of this expected phone call, so I nodded to her signaling my needed departure. Her smiling face was framed by her worried eyes. A mask we both wore in that moment.

"I have to take this," I leaned down and whispered to the student in hurried breath as I began fleeing toward the door that separated my classroom from the fifth-grade room. I remembered back later to the look of concern on the student's face which, I'm sure, mirrored mine.

As the door to my classroom shut behind me, I answered the phone, quickly taking a seat at the desk of my teacher roommate whose desk occupied the farthest end of the room. She was out for the moment, and this spot was perfect for privacy. Dr. Salydar's words to me over the phone that day remain permanently etched in my mind, as not even a *Magic Eraser* could scrub them from my memory.

"Hi Terrie. This is Dr. Salydar. I got your biopsy results back. It *is* cancer—invasive ductal carcinoma in-situ. It's grade one, which means it's slow growing, so that's good. We're not sure of the stage yet, but I'm guessing stage one or two. I'm sorry, Terrie. Do you have any questions?"

"Could you repeat all of that?" I stammered, only hearing and understanding the word, 'cancer,' out of everything she had relayed. "And, what's grade one, again? Is this curable?" I asked, my words now breaking against the waves of my tears.

As Dr. Salydar repeated it all again, now explaining what everything meant—invasive ductal carcinoma in-situ (DCIS), grade one—"when the cancer cells have grown and broken out of the breast ducts or lobules. While when the cells become invasive, they could spread to other parts of your body, this is an early and commonly detectable cancer that can be highly treatable."

But when I questioned Dr. Salydar more about what stage of cancer she believed I was in, she spoke with quiet uncertainty in her voice, and that put me in a shock that sparked me into posing the same request of her to, again, repeat everything to me. This plea was made to her three more times following.

Dr. Salydar knew shock. She worked and dealt with it every day. So, in her kind patience, she continued to repeat my diagnosis and answer my questions over and over again.

"Terrie, your chances of survival with this are very high," she said in response to my 'curable' question.

I heard the words that she had just said, but hope was not in me yet. So those reassuring words, the only reassuring words spoken, fell away from me. I stayed silent. I supposed Dr. Salydar being used to repeating herself to me a lot at this point is what led her to confidently replay those same words back regarding survival. And this time, God and Dr. Salydar made sure that I retained them, as they briefly brought me refuge in this perilous news.

Before we hung up, I asked Dr. Salydar if she would mind calling John and telling him, because I knew I would leave something out (like the whole diagnosis) or put something in that I thought was there (like, "I'm fine,") and none of it would be the truth. I knew that I also wouldn't be able to say or explain the terms as clearly as Dr. Salydar had.

"I will call him right now," she kindly replied. "Let me get his number from you. Terrie, I will have Nurse Pam get in touch with you and set up an appointment for us to meet and discuss the surgery options, and get you scheduled to see the radiation oncologist, just so you can meet her if you should need radiation following your surgery."

"Okay," I said. "Thank you, Dr. Salydar. And, thank you for calling John."

When we hung up, I pressed my face into my hands and sobbed as quietly as I could, keenly recalling my surroundings in this cloud of terror. I was completely numb. The 'heads up' of this possible diagnosis days before hadn't really helped me at all. It was *possible* then. But it was *real* now.

As I lifted my tear-soaked face from my hands, now staring into the air trying to process all that I'd been told, Lisa, my friend and teacher roommate, entered the room and approached her borrowed desk with the broken shell of me at it. Lisa knew as soon as she looked at me what had just transpired.

"I just hung up with my doctor," I explained to her, needlessly. "It's cancer," I said, as I stood to hug, or fall on, her.

Lisa was the first person I told, the one who held the

brunt of me as I absorbed the news. She is the friend whom I will always remember being the first one there after the diagnosis, holding me (I think, literally upright) and offering encouraging words to soothe the blow from the sting of the call.

After collecting myself as best I could, I made my way to the front office where I came upon another close teacher friend who was assisting at the front desk in the secretary's brief absence. As soon as I opened the door and she and I made eye contact, she knew the results. As we embraced, I quietly cried, and she began assuring me of God's presence and healing already at work. "And, speaking of work," she commented, "you should go home so you and John can be together."

"Dr. Salydar is talking to John now," I replied. "I'm going to call him in a few minutes so I can hear his voice. But I need to go pick up my fourth graders now, and I don't really want to leave. I need the kids," I said, softly. But I needed John so desperately, too. I believed that the longer I stayed at school the less real this would feel. And my colleague friend understood that.

As I passed by the office of our school principal, I stopped and tapped lightly against the door's glass window. When she opened the door and invited me in, I shared the words of my diagnosis with her. She, too, hugged me and spoke comforting God-healing sentiments. She also thought it best that I should 'call it a day.' But it was only 11:40 a.m., and I repeated to her what I'd said to my teacher friend. I really thought staying would be better for me, for now. And it turned out that I was right.

The sidewalk that led to the fourth-grade building seemed shorter than it had before as I went to pick up my twenty-one fourth grade students. This group was one of my very favorites on the day, and I looked forward to being with them every day. I had, by God's plan no doubt, arranged a week or two earlier for me and this group to be in the library today. The kids were going to delve into more literary pieces of *Lewis & Clark,* an opportunity for them to uncover new facts, becoming explorers themselves, and recording in their journals their own discoveries of this exciting expedition.

This was a perfect assignment today, because this exercise allowed the students to work independently without much assistance or instruction from me. And, there was a phone in the printer room right off the library. So, once I got the students started, I told them that I needed to make a quick phone call and would be right back. The librarian agreed to keep an eye on them while I stepped away.

I went to call John. I needed to hear him and know if he was okay. He picked up on the first ring. My tears jumped ahead of my words.

"Hi, honey," I said. "How are you?"

"How are *you*, sweetie? Are *you* okay?" John asked.

"I'm trying to be okay," I replied. "Did Dr. Salydar reach you?"

"Yes, she did. She told me everything," John said, his voice soothing and understanding.

"This is something isn't it, sweetheart?" I said, stumbling over every word.

"Yeah, it is, sweetie. But, listen, we're going to get through this, and you're going to get through this. So, make a tight fist, because I'm right there with you," John reassured.

We used to say that to each other a lot whenever something difficult was coming up or going on, we'd tell each other to 'make a tight fist.' And, when we slowly opened our hand from the tight fist, we could feel the sensation of someone holding that hand - the feeling of each other's hand clasped around our own.

"I'm right there with you, too, sweetheart," I returned. "Honey, I think I'm going to try to stay and work the day here if that's okay with you, unless you want or need for me to come home."

"No, if you feel like staying, you should. I think that would be good for you to stay in routine," John said.

John and I often thought in unison. I adore this man who's my husband, my anchor, my very best friend.

"Thanks, honey," I commented. "Well, I better go. I'll leave on time so I can get home to be with you. I really want to be with you," I said, still swimming through the tears.

"Me, too," said John. "I'll see you later. Call me again if you need or want to. I love you."

"I love you, too, honey," I replied, as we both hung up.

When I returned to the kids, they were working so hard and had gathered quite a bit of information that filled up whole pages inside their journals. As we put things away in preparation for me to return them to their classroom, one of the girls looked at me and asked if I was okay. My tear-stained face had given me away despite the many tissues that had been wiped across it numerous times.

"I'm fine, darling," I lied. "Allergies, you know."

"Wow, those must be some bad allergies," she lied back.

This girl was very intuitive and not easily fooled by anyone. And I knew that I was no exception to her instincts as I put my arm around her, exiting the library.

I went through the rest of the day with little and subtle awareness of the demanding physicalness and mental drain that was always required in my usual day. I was moving quickly as I did every day. But today, my adrenaline was pumping so hard that I could barely keep up with myself, now at the fastest of paces. And I wasn't exhausted. I was just trudging through my schedule and activities like they were nothing. No problem. No sweat. No extra fuel needed at any of my stops or pick-ups.

Fear moves you, I guess. Fear from hearing the words that you have cancer. In every moment that I was stirring and busy, the thought of cancer took a back seat. I was safe at school. In my mind for the rest of that day, my life was normal and cancer-free for as long as I was at work.

But, at the end of the day, when I walked out to leave and headed for the parking lot, there the realization was, waiting for me as I approached my car. My life wasn't mine anymore. It belonged to cancer. I had cancer.

When I finally reached home around 4 p.m., John was there waiting for me. He met me in the kitchen where we embraced and cried together for several minutes. This was our start line at the beginning of our journey together on this new, uncertain path.

As we stood there holding each other, John whispered in my ear, "You are strong. You are a warrior. You are a Navy SEAL."

And as I laughed at the thought of ever believing in any of those words, that phrase became the slogan that John repeated to me at the starting line of each new step in our walk.

9TH STOP *Loose Gravel*

JOHN PUT MOM on speaker phone as he proceeded to tell her the diagnosis of my breast cancer later that evening of the 29th. This was her first time hearing this well-kept secret that had been hushed from her ears until the passing of her birthday and our confirmation call. She took the news as I imagined she would—with disbelief, shock, fear, and tears sprinkled amidst her words. But then, her voice became grounded and mimicked quiet acceptance that I didn't expect. It was a relief and a blessing that I had not counted on but greatly needed from her.

The call to Vickie was next. And though she had received word of the possible outcome from us on April 24th, speechlessness and bewilderment still found her. The encouragement, support, and strength had been extended from Vickie 'right out of the gate' on the 24th. And, tonight was no different.

So, the way that my family had handled this news was the first real blessing, or the first one I recognized, in this ordeal. And, I was very grateful to God for the peace He had given them to transfer onto me.

When I awoke the next morning to get ready for work, it turned out that God had a lot more blessings awaiting me. And, they had been there all along, unacknowledged and disguised by my own doing.

Every day of this school year, I couldn't wait for the day to end; and now, I couldn't wait for it to begin. (I'm pretty sure that the latter is the way we're supposed to live and welcome each day.) This reminded me of the saying, 'It's not about the end. It's about the start.' This helped me focus on the start of my journey so that my mind wouldn't skip ahead to how the story might end. And, I could also sense the beginning of a new relationship with God unfolding and forming around me. I needed to know how to start this walk, and I needed Him to lead me down this unfamiliar path.

I could already feel God using my diagnosis to first open my eyes to what had been in front of me all year in my school position. God had been working to prepare me for what was ahead, unbeknownst to me, for apparently quite some time. And, He had been equipping me at this very place— my workplace—since the beginning of the school year with the spirit and strength that He knew I was going to have to possess to get through this cancer. And now, I needed to embrace that vigor, and I needed to know hope. So, God used the kids to deliver and remind me of both.

I began bottling inside myself every second that I spent with the kids, leaving me wondering how many moments I had let slip through my fingers and go fleetingly by me in my hurry just to reach the end of every day, prior to this one.

Blessings abounded around me, shaking me awake to their existence that I'd overlooked again and again. Guilt and shame overtook me. I prayed, *Lord, please forgive me for all the rocks I've thrown at my schedule and my job this year. You've had a huge boulder of blessings waiting here for me, each day, and I felt only loose gravel—tousling in my running shoes, my mind, my heart, and my soul. But I see the boulder now. And, I will keep my eyes fixed upon it here daily.*

I pondered back to when I called this job "cancer."

I compared it to having cancer. Yet the concept of the two definitions were so far apart from even residing in the same universe together, that I began to wonder what planet I could possibly have been on to think that they had a shred of commonality.

My perspective on everything was changing. I think that trials and tribulations are gentle reminders and insights from God that we don't know all we thought we did about Him, His power, His love for us, and what really matters around us in this life. I was beginning to see things as I never had before.

10ᵀᴴ STOP *One Way*

I RECEIVED A CALL from Dr. Salydar's nurse the day after my diagnosis scheduling me for a meeting to discuss the surgery options, as well as a separate appointment to meet with the radiation oncologist. So, things were happening quickly. But not to my surprise. I was quite aware of Dr. Salydar's careful attention, readiness, and genuine compassion for her patients. *Waiting* was never on her to-do list.

I was scheduled to meet with Dr. Salydar about my surgery elections the afternoon of May 6, 2014, and the radiation oncologist on May 9th. My sweet John would, of course, be with me at both.

I knew which surgery choice I was going to select, and I had discussed it with John and my family. When I was twenty-five years old and given the 99.9% probable diagnosis, I knew what I was going to do then, too.

At age twenty-five, I was going to have my left breast removed. I wanted the cancer totally out of me since just years earlier it had claimed the 38-year-old life of my father. I didn't think about reconstruction then. Or, I didn't know much about it. But I was spared from that positive diagnosis at that young age, where the hand of God was already at the wheel.

Now, at age forty-nine, I was older and more informed

about what each surgery option entailed. And I knew about reconstruction. But, after having mammograms for twenty-two years, sometimes every six months within that time period, and always watching the left breast, but having cancer now in the right one, I knew what I wanted to do. I wanted a bilateral mastectomy without reconstruction, because I didn't want to feel this fear and uncertainty as I had for so many years, ever again. I didn't want cancer to sneak up or blend in behind another figure in my breasts, and I didn't want to have any more mysteries and maybes. I would wear prosthetics. *Hmm . . . I wondered if I could pick my size—like a lot of sizes down from what I am!* That was my first light-hearted thought on this pilgrimage.

I had discussed my decision with so many. Except God. What was I thinking? As I lay in bed a few nights before my meeting with Dr. Salydar, I prayed to God and gave it to Him to decide. And I prayed that I would have an open mind in every offering that Dr. Salydar and I discussed. I wanted and needed God to tell me what to do and follow *His* plan.

He didn't wait long to answer. Maybe a minute or two had passed since my "Amen." My eyes fell toward the closed bedroom door, lit from the silhouette of our dresser lantern, as I heard God speak, "You know what to do. You've always known what to do, so go and do it. Follow your heart on this."

So, this was my *One Way* . . . God's way, and the only way I needed to tread.

God was evidenced to me larger than He ever had been before on that night. I knew He was with me, because I could feel Him from the very beginning of this journey. But, for me to hear His words in whispers were something I had never expected or imagined I would experience. And, I didn't know it yet, but this was the start of many more signs and whispers I would receive from Him.

On Tuesday, May 6th, Dr. Salydar greeted me and John at the door to her office as she had the last two visits. She led John and me to a conference room where we would, first, watch a video explaining various types of breast cancer and the advancement of surgery and treatment options for them.

John had been trying for a week to get me to watch some informational videos that he had discovered in his own research of my diagnosis via the internet. This was actually a quest he had begun immediately following his phone call from Dr. Salydar announcing my cancer. But I couldn't bring myself to watch or hear about my cancer on a screen leading into the worldwide web of scary, and maybe, inaccurate and confusing data. Even though, I was certain that anything John found would be accurate and helpful. Despite John's many soft attempts in the reassurances of comfort that watching these videos would provide me, I refused. I had my own internal projector playing 24/7, and I couldn't shut that off. But I could stay away from other venues. Until now, that is, as I sat beside John in Dr. Salydar's office watching her press the *play* button to begin a video. John looked at me with an endearing smile and a wink as he reached for my hand. *So much for my boycotting watching any breast cancer videos,* I thought out loud to myself and to John.

In retrospect, the video was a wealth of information from diagrams, medical advances, survival rates, options with explanations, and guidance in dealing with cancer, to pictures of some of the post surgeries. It even showed what invasive ductal cancer, (my cancer), looked like inside of the breast. The cells appeared as little beans falling out of a tube (duct). And, while the bean cells were contained within the breast, it was startling to see them pouring out into the breast wall on the diagram. My first thought was, *have these spread in me?* But God quickly replaced that thought with what I had been told by Dr. Salydar earlier. "Slow growing, and survival rate with this type of cancer is very high."

"Breathe," I whispered to myself, as John's hand tightened around mine.

As I sat there trying to take my eyes off the screen, while having them almost glued to it at the same time, told me that this was a *showing* ordered by God to prepare me for the surgery discussion ahead. This was the visual keyhole of what I would look like, the care I would need to take, and the emotional and physical effects that would come with a bilateral mastectomy.

The video had not been over long before Dr. Salydar re-entered the room. This video not only provoked some questions inside me, it gave me the open mind that I had prayed for upon entering into the surgical conversation.

Dr. Salydar was a daily host at this table, and as soon as she sat down and looked at me, she asked, "So, what questions do you have?"

Pushing back my tears, I asked, "Because my cancer is an invasive one depicting all the cells dumping out of the duct, does that mean those cells have spread to other places outside my breast?"

"They could, but I don't believe in your case, they have. Yours is a grade one, slow-growing cancer which could also imply that it's been caught early. Your cancer shows that it's contained within your breast, so I wouldn't worry about the cells traveling at all, because we have no indication of that at this time. I will, however, know more about that during the surgery, because we will give you a dye injection the day before your surgery that will light up the passageway in your lymph system to the area of your cancer. That passageway will direct me toward which lymph nodes to remove to be tested for any stray cells. Women used to have 33+ lymph nodes removed for precautionary measures, and at the operating surgeon's discretion, because we didn't have the advances and research that we have now that can, literally, light the way for us to know which and how many lymph nodes to take. And sometimes it's only one or two, which makes it so much easier for the patient's healing, lessens the chance of developing lymphedema, and we don't have all these wasted lymph nodes that were taken out for safety's sake that needed to remain untouched, because they were untouched by the cancer. There will be a Surgery Stage Report following your surgery that will provide detailed information of all the findings that will help us to determine the treatment options as well."

"Wow. Okay," I replied, breathlessly processing all that she had said, while also finding myself dumbfounded by her keen awareness of the other questions I was going to ask but hadn't yet.

She had covered most, if not all, of the answers within her reply to my one question. No, Dr. Salydar was not a novice to breast cancer theatrics, and that apparently included the list of questions filed inside of a woman's mind after viewing this reel.

In her hand, Dr. Salydar held several copies of the pathology report outlining my complete cancer diagnosis that she, then, passed out to John and me. She thoughtfully and carefully interpreted every section of the report. My estrogen and progesterone receptors were positive, and the Her2 was negative. Those were good alignments, and Dr. Salydar was very happy with those diagnostic readings.

Once we finished our review of the pathology results with

her, she flipped our copy over revealing the blank back of the stapled sheets. It was time to discuss the surgery options.

Dr. Salydar profiled each as she wrote down the options at hand, listing their statistics and outcomes. "A lumpectomy," she explained, "will provide you breast conservation and has a 7% risk of local recurrence over 15 years. A mastectomy, is, of course, the removal of the breast and has a 2-3% risk of recurrence. So, the percentage rates are not that far apart from each other in the choices, and there is no difference in survival."

Where is the bilateral mastectomy option? I wondered, as I stared down at what Dr. Salydar had charted in front of me on the only two choices she had listed.

"Is a bilateral out of the question?" I asked, curiously. "I was kind of leaning toward that because of all the years of mysteries and wonder surrounding my breasts."

Dr. Salydar reached for a new blank sheet of paper lying on the table in front of her. "Well, let's talk about your family history beginning on your father's side," she commented.

"Daddy died of lung cancer at the age of thirty-eight," I began. "The cancer actually started in his lung and moved to his liver."

"Wait," Dr. Salydar interrupted. "Cancer doesn't move like that, from lung to liver. It had to begin somewhere else in his body and then travel to those organs from its origin. Was your father treated for anything else before his cancer diagnosis that you can remember?"

"Yes," I recalled. "He had a small raised bump the size of a marble on the side of his neck a year or so before his diagnosis. He went to our general practitioner, and he gave Daddy some medicine to shrink and clear it. Whatever the doctor gave him must have worked, because it was gone in no time."

"Oh, Terrie," said Dr. Salydar, apologetically. "It didn't go away; it moved. Your father had lymphoma. It can look and start as a growth on the neck, just as you described. And, when it moves and is no longer visible to the naked eye, it has just relocated; usually, to one of the breasts. And from the breast, it moves to the lung, and then, to the liver. So, that was the path of your father's cancer. He had lymphoma."

"Really? Are you sure?" I stuttered, my words bumping into each other.

Then, I remembered that I had heard this before. Mom had, in previous years, told our family doctor about the growth on Daddy's neck, and he had deduced the same diagnosis. Lymphoma. From this point, we continued to peel back the bark of my family's bountiful cancer tree.

Dr. Salydar sketched out the information and scenario of every branch, gathering from one and connecting it to the other as she drafted along. And, by the time we were done, not leaving one leaf of any limb unturned, Dr. Salydar looked at me and said, "Terrie, if you want to do the bilateral, let's do it. With your family's history, and if you're on board, I think that's the best option for you."

For a moment I was struck speechless. With the quick impression of a pencil tracing out two trees, a bilateral mastectomy was a choice. *What just happened?* I thought to myself, now dealing with the reality of that wanting. Then it hit me—God happened! God had led this entire meeting. A choice that wasn't even on Dr. Salydar's original list was now 'the best option.' And, only God could have orchestrated the *overture* leaves to the *postlude* of His will, and ultimately, my wish. God . . . the unbelievably believable conductor of our lives!

At my realization of God's presence at the table, my words flowed, "I'm on board," I said, confidently.

I looked over at John who had remained quiet, with the exception of his questions every now and then, throughout the meeting. "What do you think, honey?" I asked.

"I think it sounds like a good plan. I'm going to support whatever you want to do," he replied, sincerely.

"Are you going to want reconstruction?" Dr. Salydar asked me.

"No. I want to wear prosthetics," I said, without hesitation.

"That's great," Dr. Salydar remarked. "You will not be in near as much pain and discomfort, as sometimes, reconstruction can bring. And, your surgery time will not be as long, either. You'll probably be in surgery around three hours, as opposed to the seven hours reconstruction can take."

"Wow, I didn't know that," I replied.

"Well, unless you have anything else you want to discuss, Terrie, I'll send Nurse Pam in, and we'll get your surgery scheduled," Dr. Salydar commented.

"Let's do it." I said, with both hands, both feet, and both breasts, all in.

John and I extended our hands and hugs of appreciation to Dr. Salydar as she prepared to leave the room. I was in wonderful hands—God's and Dr. Salydar's.

When Nurse Pam came in, she had already made a phone call to the hospital to schedule the surgery date. A tentative date of May 22nd, just two weeks and two days from today, was planned. Nurse Pam told us that several doctors share the morning slots in booking the surgery unit. And, if there was an overlap of additional time needed for a surgery that shifted into the morning of the 22nd, my surgery date would then move to May 29th, a week later. She said that she would call to convey which date as soon as she had confirmation.

When a week had passed by and I still hadn't heard

anything, with anxiety getting the best of me, I called Nurse Pam and was, indeed, confirmed for the date of May 22nd. In her own excitement, Nurse Pam believed that she had transposed the numbers on the phone pad when she called me days earlier to inform me of the definitive date.

I was glad that the surgery was going to happen so soon. I hadn't expected a May date at all, but I did expect that as the time drew nearer, my apprehension and imagination would join forces and stir up some good, old-fashioned, completely natural, fear—'False Expectations Appearing Real.'

It's so easy for our minds to enlarge our circumstances. But God scouts out the territory ahead of us where our feet are to tread long before we arrive. So, He knows what awaits us in advance; and therefore, prepares us accordingly.

11TH STOP Buckle Up for Safety (Look Up for Hope)

THE DAYS LEADING up to my surgery were ones wrapped tightly around the kids at school. The students provided me therapy greater and richer than any money could buy. Their lessons in laughter, loving every day, youthful wisdom, perseverance, and resilience made their therapy priceless. And, their lessons contained the very ingredients, I discovered later, that were needed to fight cancer.

The kids were like a seatbelt that kept me still, safe, and protected from the imagined ride that this disease threatened to take me on. They kept me strapped in place and firmly secure from my own thoughts of the unthinkable. In my mind, and even in my body, my cancer didn't seem to exist when I was around the kids. And the children never knew about that monster inside me that they were helping me to conquer every minute I was with them.

Because my surgery was on May 22nd, my last day at school would be May 19th. And, as the day approached that I was going to have to tell the students that 'I was graduating three weeks earlier from the school year than they,' I met with Mrs. Clinedinst, the assistant principal, to share with her the message I was going to relay to them.

I had thought about what I was going to say to the kids as I lay in bed a few nights earlier, my words in a debate among themselves. And in my cluttered thoughts, God swept in and offered these words as my announcement, "Guys, I'm going to have to graduate three weeks earlier than you this school year. And, believe me, it's not because I'm smarter than you, because you all defy that, everyday! I need to have some surgery that will require some lengthy recovery time, so while I won't be back this year, I will definitely be back with you again next year."

God even took care of giving me the thoughtful answer to an inevitable question that one of the students was sure to ask: "What kind of surgery are you having, Mrs. Childress?"

God's response, "Oh, it's a surgery that adults need to have sometimes, and now, it's my turn."

I knew, or I thought I did, whom the very student was who would pose that question. It was a girl who was always full of questions, and sometimes, answers. But, when the question came, it wasn't from her mouth, but instead, from the inquisitive tongue of a quiet fifth grade girl who rarely spoke in front of a class unless spoken to, or required to, for an assignment. Following my God-given response, the girl simply replied back, as she shrugged her shoulders, "Okay."

Mrs. Clinedinst and I were equally happy with those words and ideas that weren't mine. And, we both agreed that the kids didn't need to know that I had cancer. It would just have worried and upset them, and there was no need for that. They were in the middle of SOL testing and preparing for a happy, well-deserved ending to their hardworking school year. They didn't need any distractions clouding the anxiety and excitement of either one of those important events. And selfishly, I needed them to remain the therapists that they had no idea they were for me.

I told the fourth and fifth graders of my early departure a week before my last day. While relaying the news to fifth grade went very smoothly, telling the fourth grade was quite difficult. I had grown particularly close with the students in this grade level, largely due to the history we already had together in their younger years when I worked with them in reading.

I had just finished reading two chapters of the book, *Flora and Ulysses*, to Mrs. Martin's fourth graders, as was our daily routine in closing our reading period. Mrs. Martin then cued me to go ahead with my farewell message, and as the fourth graders sat huddled on the floor with anxious eyes and open ears wondering what I was about to announce, I began with God's script. But, the more I spoke, the more my words became gagged by my tears, my voice shaky and broken as I uttered the last line of God's notice.

Mrs. Martin walked over and put her arm around me, which calmed and transported me into a more light-hearted realm, as I began joking with the kids in Flora's cynical voice. "Now, see?" I gestured with a pointing finger. "My graduation brings tears to my eyes just as yours will to you. So, tears are inevitable when you're about to graduate and venture onto a new path," I performed through my smiling teeth.

Praise the good Lord, the room became filled with booming laughter, as the kids got up to hug me and wish me well. I think that one of them even congratulated me on my graduation!

While I wished I hadn't begun to cry, I remembered that when God has a task for us, He never promises that it's going to be easy. My original line of thinking was that since God had given me the words to say to the children, that the hard part was done. I had the words. But even though God had given me the words to say, my voice had to be the one to speak them. And my mind didn't acknowledge that role until it was time for me to act. What's easy for God isn't meant to be easy for us. But He gives us what we need when we need it—like when the outstretched arm of Mrs. Martin around me turned me into the character of Flora from the story we had been group reading. Who knew God would put me into Flora's shoes? I never saw that coming, and that's exactly how God works! We don't see Him coming because He's always there.

I mentioned in an earlier chapter that God used the kids to deliver both strength and hope to me. Here's how He used His young messengers. He gave me endless opportunities to observe the innocent nature that encompasses children and allows them to capture and make every moment count like a snapshot frozen in time. I got to look into their eyes (windows) of daily happiness, sheer curiosity, and witness their ability of not taking things, or themselves, too seriously. For life is too short for that. These were the building blocks of strength and hope that the kids laid out right before my eyes. It was a 'work in progress' I had missed, or simply not *seen*, until now.

"The world says that 'seeing is believing,' but God wants us to believe in order to see. The psalmist said he would have despaired unless he had 'believed that he would see' the goodness of the Lord in the land of the living."—Psalm 27:13, NIV Streams in the Desert.

The fourth and fifth graders were 'the land of the living' for me. God's smallest examples of how He wants us to live and why life is so worth our *seeing* (believing)!

12TH STOP Objects in Mirror are Closer Than They Appear

I DUSTED THE HOUSE and cleaned the bathrooms the last weekend before my surgery. And as my polish-treated rag scooted across the wooden tables and my wet sudsy sponge swept around the bathroom tub, I wondered if I would be able to clean like this after my surgery without my breasts. *Hmm . . . that could be another upswing to this. Not having to clean. I wonder if John would see it as an upswing,* I chuckled to myself.

Washing the laundry and packing were next on my list. John and I were going to stay in a hotel on the campus of the hospital the night before my surgery and several nights following so I would be close in case there were any complications upon my hospital discharge. Surprisingly, when you have a bilateral mastectomy, you only spend one night in the hospital unless the doctor, of course, deems it necessary for further monitoring, pain management, or other arising circumstances.

I packed three bags: one for the hotel with my and John's clothes and toiletries; one for me to take to the hospital that, among the usual small items, cargoed an endearing stuffed dog named Dublin from John's cousin, Ken, a small stand-up sign from my Aunt Faye and Uncle Randy that read, "Hello.

This is God. I will be handling all of your problems and concerns today. That's my job. Your job is to give them to me, and then to trust me. Have a great day!", and a pink flower-shaped pillow that Vickie and Kevin had given me for extra cushioning while riding in the car following my surgery; then, there was a bag of special books—the *NIV Streams in the Desert* Bible from John, a word search activity book, and a book entitled, *An Invisible Thread.*

Besides the obvious uses, many of these items held special meaning and purpose for me, which is why I packed them. The Bible was going to be read by John and me at the hotel the night before my surgery and kept on the nightstand by my side of the bed for reading and reassurance when I returned from my hospital stay. Dublin, the stuffed dog, was going to share the hospital bed with me to bring me security, smiles, and softness. The flower-shaped pillow was going to be my comfortable ride back to the hotel following my hospital discharge. And, the small stand-up sign carrying the message from God was going to be placed on the table beside my hospital bed so that when I woke up from my surgery, it would be there for me to read. Over and over again.

After the housework, laundry, and packing were all done, John and I met Jim and Sharon for dinner the night before we were to leave the next morning. It was a bittersweet meal that I don't remember biting into that much. I wasn't particularly hungry, so my plate became a painting palette where I just swirled one food group into the other. A real artist may have found some value in the kaleidoscope of neutral colors that my mixing had brought about.

Sharon, having gone through breast cancer herself years earlier, knew the anxiety I was feeling, the thoughts I was thinking, and the questions of what I would be like and look like on the other side of this surgery. So, when she looked at me from across the table and asked how I was doing she was quite familiar and relative to my response.

"The normalcy," I began, "the routine I had at school has passed. My time and therapy sessions," I announced, light-heartedly, "with the kids has ended, and the work that was awaiting me at home is done. There's nothing for me to hide behind or keep me busy anymore. So now, I have to face it. This cancer and surgery are the only things on my calendar now. And I'm scared to death," my words, all at once, being swallowed up by my streaming tears.

"I know," Sharon replied, reaching over for my hand. "But you're going to get through this, and it's going to be over before you know it."

"Define 'over before you know it,'" I squeaked out, jokingly.

We giggled, and that seemed to halt my tears for the time being.

For the rest of our meal, the conversation was as normal as it could be, and there were more moments of laughter poured into the sweetness of our time together.

As we walked out of the restaurant, Jim and Sharon directed us toward their car. Opening their hatchback, they pulled out a large tote full of wrapped gifts and handed it to me.

"What in the world?" I said in surprise. "What's all this? You all are too much! This is too much!"

"It's not all from us," Sharon commented. "When I had my cancer surgery, a friend of mine gave me a care package like this, full of gifts from several different people. And, I was told to open a gift whenever I was feeling low and needed a pick-me-up. So, when you have those moments when you're feeling down, just reach in and unwrap a gift to give you some cheer."

For several seconds, I was speechless and overwhelmed by this extraordinary kindness. I could tell that John was, too, as he looked down at the bag and glanced up at Jim and Sharon in amazement.

My weeping consumed my words again as I began to speak, "Thank you all SO much. This is so incredibly sweet. I can't believe you did this. I'm so touched."

I think it's fair to say that Jim agreed completely with the last thing I said, but not the way I meant it. "Now, listen, Terrie," he remarked, "don't be looking for something in that bag from me, because you won't find anything in there from me," Jim teased.

"Oh, c'mon, Jim," I returned, jestingly. "Are you kidding me? I can't believe that. There's still time for you to toss something in, if you'd like," I said, holding the bag out in front of him.

"Forget it, Terrie," he shot back, laughing.

Laughter filled the air around us as we hugged and said our good-byes for the evening.

Their bag of gifts would be the fourth bag now going along with John and me tomorrow, as we placed it on the floorboard of the car behind my seat. But the best things we were taking with us weren't things. They were the precious words and gestures of love expressed by our family and friends. And they were meticulously packed inside our hearts and permanently folded into our memories.

13TH STOP *No U Turn*

As we pulled out of our driveway to head for Charlottesville the morning of May 21, 2014, we were met by our neighbor, Larry, who was outside working in his yard. He drove his mower over to John's side of the car to wish us well and let us know that we would be in his prayers. And then, Larry lowered his head, looking over at me in the passenger seat and said something to me that I'll never forget.

"The Lord is going to bless you, Terrie. I know He is, and you need to know that, too," Larry assuredly proclaimed.

"Thank you, Larry. I appreciate that so much. Thank you," I replied, my eyes and voice crescendoing up to tears.

I wanted to say so much more to Larry than 'Thank you.' I wanted to ask him, "How do you know that? Did God tell you that? Did He speak to you, because He's spoken to me, but I haven't heard Him say *that*?"

But I don't think God was supposed to relay that message to me Himself. He gave that job to Larry, one of his full-time faithful servants. So, God sent our trusted friend and neighbor to carry out this message for Him so that I would be sure to receive it, and, remember it.

Larry's words from God replayed in my mind often during my cancer journey when I would come to a crossroads, or a dark tunnel, that I didn't see up ahead until I was sitting right in front of it.

On our drive to Charlottesville, I sat looking out the window feeling the realness of the surgery I was facing. There was no turning the car around as ironically indicated by a *No U Turn* sign up ahead. The only way out was through. I had to go through this to get out of it.

After John and I checked into our hotel room, we went to grab a buffet-style lunch. But just as I sat down with my plate, my phone rang with the area code of Charlottesville blinking on its screen. When I answered, it was the anesthesiologist nurse calling with pre-surgery questions and procedures. The loudness of the restaurant drowned out our conversation with large waves of voluminous voices that crashed into every word we spoke. I excused myself to John, and the nurse, as I headed outside for a more low-tide discussion.

Once outside, I was greeted by a cloud of smoke coming from several long white lit sticks hanging from mouths of a crowd. *Oh well,* I thought. *I already have cancer, so what can these do to me for the next five to ten minutes?* Not really wanting to know the answer, I moved to a bench hidden by a brick wall that the prowling smoke never found.

When asked what questions or concerns I had, I informed the nurse that anesthesia usually makes me quite sick, causing me to vomit at least once, and often, more than that. She made note and said she would be sure to pass that along to the anesthesiologist so he could 'provide precautions to, hopefully, prevent that.'

Then, I brought up a big concern—to me, that is. One that had been worrying me for a while.

"I've never taken off my wedding band," I told the nurse. "In past surgeries that I've had, a staff member has always just wrapped a strip of white first-aid tape around my ring so that the metal doesn't compromise the surgery. Can you all do that, too?"

"Mrs. Childress," she responded, kindly, "I think you will want to take your wedding ring off this time. With the mastectomy you're having, there will be a lot of equipment in the operating room with you that can put you at high risk of being burned if you have any metal on your body whatsoever. I don't want that to happen to you, and I really don't think you should take that risk. The choice is, of course, yours, but I think you need to leave your ring at home."

I sighed out an, "Okay, thanks," as we hung up.

I couldn't leave my ring at home. I wasn't at home. And I couldn't leave it at the hotel. That wouldn't be a safe place even though it was a safe hotel. There was nowhere I could leave my ring.

I returned to the table with my appetite gone. I didn't have much to begin with, but now I was full without ever taking a bite. As I slid back into the booth, John looked at me and asked if everything was alright. "Yes," I lied. "I'm sorry I was gone so long. The nurse had a lot of pre-registration questions, and I had one for her."

"Well, you eat, and take your time," John urged, his plate already empty.

"I'm not even hungry, honey," I said. "I'm ready to go when you are."

"You need to eat something, even if it's just a little bit," he replied. "Go get a fresh, hot plate of food."

I pushed my now, cold plate to the side of the table and got up to get a fresh one, topped with a few mashed potatoes, green beans, and a roll. *I wonder who's going to eat this?* I thought, as I looked down at my new hot plate. But John was right. I needed to eat something to strengthen my body, if for no other reason. My body was going to be going through something that I couldn't even fathom, so denying it food was not a smart choice.

I ate what I could before we headed out the door. When we got into the car, I began telling John what the nurse had said about the risk of me wearing my wedding band during surgery. This frightened John, and he wasn't willing for me to take the 'burning' risk.

"Sweetie, you have to take it off," he said, without hesitation or entertaining the idea of further discussion. "It's not worth it."

"But I don't have anywhere to put it where it will be safe," I said, pleading my case. "I don't want to just put it in a suitcase."

"I know where it will be safe," John quickly replied. "On *my* finger. I'll wear your ring on my finger. It will be on me the whole time, and I'll keep it on until you can wear it again."

"*You'll* wear it?" I said, getting used to and loving the idea at the same time. "Will it fit you?"

"It will fit my pinky finger, for sure, and maybe another finger," John planned. "I'll try it on in the morning and wear it on the finger that it's most secure around and can't slide off."

I looked over at him, as he took my hand. "You're on, sweetheart," I said. "You're brilliant, you know. I married a brilliant man."

"You know, you're the only one who thinks that," John said.

"No, you just think I'm the only one. But many others think it, too," I remarked, reflectively.

John kissed my hand. *That was the handshake on the deal,* I thought to myself.

We were on our way to a three o'clock dye injection appointment that Dr. Salydar had scheduled for me at the hospital. The injection point of entry would occur near the cancer site in my right breast to help guide Dr. Salydar during the surgery, taking her through the pathway of the lymph system so she would know which lymph node(s) to remove and test. The dye would, literally, light the way for her, and 'the lymph nodes that were lit' were the very ones that Dr. Salydar would extract.

Just before the nurse penetrated my skin with the four-pronged dye injection needle, she told me that it would feel like a bee sting. I told her that, believe it or not, I'd never been stung by a bee. We had just finished laughing at that fact when she gave me the, "Ready?" and proceeded to 'sting' the outer side of my right breast. If that was what a bee sting felt like, I never wanted to be stung by one.

"Wow," I responded, as the 'stinger' came out, "that was a BIG bee!"

"Oh, I'm so sorry," the nurse said, sympathetically. "That can be more painful than it looks. And, everyone feels it differently. But most women say that 'it feels like a bee sting,' so that's my interpretation to others."

"Well, I guess they would know since they've been stung by a bee before. So, bless their hearts for giving the rest of us a 'heads up' on that," I replied, now loathing all bees.

Later that evening, John and I stopped at Quiznos to have a small sandwich for supper. Phone calls from my family followed our meal, as well as a call from a teacher friend who had just learned that my surgery was tomorrow, as she thought it was scheduled for a later date.

It was great to talk with all of them. And they all had the same two questions for me: "How are you? Are you okay?"

Though while I answered them that, "I was scared, but okay," I felt this surge of calming peace come over me at the same time, that was beyond my realm of understanding. This peace allowed me the opportunity to even joke some with my family, reassuring them that I was, indeed, fine. And, I knew that this peace was God blocking out any fear, any doubt or reservation, and every worry from my mind and mouth—a revelation of His true presence with and around me.

This was the feeling that the rest of the evening provided me. Every time I felt just a twinge of fear creeping up, it was immediately quelled with an overwhelming calmness and strength that were not from my own being or doing.

John and I read the Bible that he had bought for me as we sat across from each other on the bed. God's word that night to us read, "*There is a divine mystery in suffering, one that has a strange and supernatural power and has never been completely understood by human reason. No one has ever developed a deep level of spirituality or holiness without experiencing a great deal of suffering. When a person who suffers reaches a point where he can be calm and carefree, inwardly smiling at his own suffering, then the suffering has accomplished its blessed ministry.*

It is in this experience of complete suffering that the Holy Spirit works many miraculous things deep within our soul. In this condition, our entire being lies perfectly still under the hand of God; every power and ability of the mind, will, and heart are at last submissive; a quietness of eternity settles into the entire soul; and finally, the mouth becomes quiet, having only a few words to say. At this point the person stops imagining castles in the sky and pursuing foolish ideas, and his reasoning becomes calm and relaxed, with all choices removed, because the only choice has now become the purpose of God.

Oh, the blessings of absolute submission to Christ! What a blessing to lose our own strength, wisdom, plans and desires (like worry) and to be where every ounce of our being becomes like a peaceful Sea of Galilee under the omnipotent feet of Jesus!"—L.B. Cowman, NIV Streams in the Desert.

So, that's why I have this unexplainable peace inside me, I thought—an unexplainable peace that God had just thoroughly explained in the reading of His word. And this peace that I was clothed in was so apparent to John on this night before my surgery.

As I lay in bed wide awake until one o'clock in the morning 'imagining castles in the sky and pursuing foolish thoughts and ideas' that God's written word had addressed and been against, my fears tried to challenge the Holy Spirit. But fear lost, as my body and mind returned to the calm reassurance of the Lord.

I looked over at John, who was now sound asleep, as I'm sure he thought I was. And as I stared at him, I started thinking about the best day of my life. That was easy, I thought. The day I became John's wife . . . and every day after.

14TH STOP *Under Construction*

THE ALARM CLOCK awakened the fear inside me to its 6:00 a.m. calling. John was already up and showered. I guessed he hadn't slept the whole night through, either. The peace I had felt last night still encompassed me, but fear was in the corner of that peaceful place this morning, and I couldn't help but wonder how things were going to go today, the day of my surgery. It was Thursday, May 22, 2014.

I was numb when I climbed into the shower, realizing that this was the last time I would see my body this way in a shower. As my washcloth cleansed over my breasts, I couldn't imagine what I would look like without them. I shaved my legs last night in a bath and my arms this morning, because I didn't know when I might be able to do that again. And, I loaded on the deodorant, fully aware that it was going to be wiped from me before my surgery. But I didn't know when I would be able to wear deodorant again, either, so I needed that to *stick* for a while.

I was worried about John, and he was worried about me. We embraced and held each other for several moments before we left the hotel room, exchanging words of reassurance back and forth to each other, praying, and feeling God with us both.

My surgery was scheduled for 9:30 a.m., so John and I had to be at the hospital by 7:30 a.m. The one-minute ride over to the hospital from the campus hotel was not long enough. And when John parked the car in the parking garage and we got out, I was trying to direct my attention and move my thoughts toward things—other cars, people, and conversations—happening around us. I was trying to feel a normal day in front of me that was anything but.

As John and I sat in the waiting area for my name to be called, we held hands, and he began to slowly slip off the wedding band from my finger. He tried it on his third finger, but the ring was too small. When he slid it onto his left pinky finger right beside his own wedding band, it was a snug yet perfect fit. I laid my head on his shoulder with happy tears now streaming down, as I gazed at his hand carrying the symbols of our love side by side. It was a beautiful irony and another subtle reminder from God that John and I were going to get through this together, side by side.

A moment later, John's phone vibrated a text. It was Vickie. She wanted to know how I was. John snapped a picture of my tearful smile and sent it to her with the words, "She's nervous. But 'she is strong. She is a warrior. She is a Navy SEAL.'" John's infamous and humorous slogan, now at the threshold of my surgery.

Vickie texted back a sweet message. The key role I mentioned earlier that Vickie would be playing later in my journey was debuting today. John had asked her a few weeks earlier if she would call members on my side of the family once he had contacted her following my surgery, to let them all know that I was out of surgery and how it went. John had a long list of people—the church, the school, our friends, and his side of the family—that he was going to contact, and he knew that he couldn't stay on his phone indefinitely and get too tied up. Though this request that he made of Vickie would have originally been 'out of her comfort zone,' she quickly accepted and agreed to make the family calls. She wore these shoes very well, I was told, with great finesse and perfect posturing.

"Mrs. Childress," was the next sound that vibrated. Though this call was from the voice of a nurse. I remained seated, or frozen, for a second to see if there was another Mrs. Childress who was going to respond. But, when John stood up, he blew my cover.

As I approached the nurse, she said, "Hi, Mrs. Childress. My name is Stacy. How are you today?"

"I think I'm okay, Stacy. How are you?" I replied, as I patted her on the back like we were old friends.

"I'm fine. It looks like it's going to be a nice day outside," Stacy remarked.

"Yes, it does," I said, yearning so much to be on the outside.

Stacy looked over at me as we neared the prep room. "You smell good," she commented.

"Thanks, it's my deodorant." (Yeah, I'd put on enough that it could easily have been mistaken for perfume.)

We laughed, and she said, "Well, that's great-smelling deodorant!"

I think that was the only time we laughed as the surgery prep began to unfold. Stacy had given me a Benadryl. This was to help with inflammation from the surgery and also assist in keeping my body restful. But my veins had trouble accepting the IV, and I began sweating profusely and looked up at John to tell him that I thought I was going to be sick. He ran over to the sink and grabbed the sick bowl, and I threw up the Benadryl just ten minutes after Stacy had given it to me. I wondered how swollen and restful my body would be now.

The anesthesiologist had entered the room right before my inflicted sickness to introduce himself. He then proceeded to ask me some questions, but I was unable to respond as I began to faint in my bed.

When I regained consciousness, I was told that an IV therapist would be coming shortly to get my IV started. And she did. She came and got the IV in, easily and painlessly, at first try.

It was 9:40 a.m. when Dr. Salydar came into the room. She apologized for her tardiness as she and I clasped hands. I didn't mind that she was late. I was in no hurry. She, John, and I spoke just briefly before she headed to meet me in the O.R. The hands of God resting upon the hands of Dr. Salydar gave me the perfect surgical team!

It was time for me to kiss my sweet John and tell him to 'make a tight fist' as they wheeled me toward the operating room. Once inside, the assisting operating nurse untied my hospital gown and started wiping my chest and armpits down. *And there goes the deodorant,* I thought. *Hey, she missed some!* I quickly and happily realized. Maybe those missed patches would be enough to get me through smelling okay for the next couple of days. Or not.

Dr. Salydar walked in, dressed for the occasion, just seconds before the anesthesiologist told me to think of my favorite place as he held the anesthesia mask above my mouth.

"Williamsburg!" I replied, excitedly.

"Great!" the anesthesiologist echoed back, also with excitement. "Now, go to your favorite spot there."

"Merchants Square," I commented, picturing it before the mask even touched my face. But the mask must have already been on my face, because just as soon as I mentioned the Square, that's where I was transported—standing on the brick-laid sidewalk, with my purse in hand, right in front of the best shops in town.

I must be dreaming, my mind wearily thought, *because I*

don't have any bags in my hands. I always had at least one or two bags of treasures that I'd found on the Square. But my hands were unfurnished. This seemed more like John's dream than mine. He would love for me to leave Merchants Square empty-handed, if only just once.

I started to hear unfamiliar sounds around me that didn't mimic the tunes of fifes and drums on Merchants Square. These were clamors of rolling machines on wheels, metal cabinets being closed, and loud clanging tools. As I groggily attempted to open my eyes, I realized that my time on Merchants Square had, indeed, just been a dream. I was back to reality. And I quickly remembered where this reality was, as I began uncontrollably asking anyone within earshot, "Am I cancer-free? Am I cancer-free?"

A joyful response came immediately from a very happy Recovery Room nurse named Amy.

"Hi! I'm Amy! Can you hear me?" she asked.

"Amy, am I cancer-free?" I repeated.

"Yes," she said. "And, you did so well."

As I began slipping back into sleep, I wondered, *what did that mean? What did I do so well?*

When my eyes opened briefly, again, I saw the image of Dr. Salydar standing over me. "Hi, Terrie," she said, softly.

"Dr. Salydar, am I cancer-free?" I chirped out.

"Everything went well. You did so well," she said. But that wasn't a yes. *Was* it?

The anesthesia tugged at my consciousness again as I continued going in and out. But each time that I came to, if even for a few seconds, I would awake asking the same question, "Am I cancer-free?" I think I even asked and answered myself once.

When I arrived at my assigned hospital room, I remember dreaming that I was on an airplane as the nurses were lifting me out of one bed into another. And I heard myself remark, "Oh, I'm going to be sick."

John told me later that my saying that alerted them to grab for the sick pan, whereas I did get sick, still in my groggy state. Who knew? (God knew.) I thought it was just motion sickness from the airplane ride.

When I finally fully awoke from the anesthesia, John was sitting on the couch beside my bed. I smiled at him, and then, my eyes went to the clock on the wall behind him. It was 4:40 p.m. The last time I had looked at a clock, it was 9:40 a.m. *Where have I been all this time*, I nervously wondered. A thin blanket with a sheet was covering me, though my eyes never looked directly at my chest area. I was grateful to be covered.

John got up and kissed my forehead. "How are you, sweetie?" he asked, softly.

"I'm okay, honey," I replied. But I couldn't help myself. I had to ask my sweetheart, and I knew he would tell me the truth. "Am I cancer-free?" I begged.

"Yes, sweetie. Dr. Salydar said that everything went really well. She got the cancer. And, she only had to remove one lymph node. You're going to be fine."

My eyes welled up with tears of relief, joy, and a twinge of uncertainty for what could be up ahead. But apparently, I was cancer-free. And at this moment, that's all that really mattered to me.

"How are *you*, sweetheart?" I asked John. I knew that his day had been more difficult, long, and unnerving than mine. And he had been awake for every second of it.

"I'm fine," he replied, with a grin. "I'm just fine."

Suddenly, a nurse entered the room to welcome me awake and check my vitals.

"How are you feeling?" she asked.

"Well, I'm not in any pain right now," I commented. "But I do have to go to the bathroom. Can I get up for that, or no?"

"I will have to get some other nurses to help me get you up if you feel like you can walk to the bathroom," she said. "We will need to be careful though, because you have four drainage tubes hanging from your chest and upper abdomen near your rib cage."

"I do?" I said, surprised and panicked.

John immediately jumped in. "Sweetie, Dr. Salydar thought she was only going to put two or three tubes in, but she decided to insert four so that your incision could drain faster."

"Oh, so that's good, then," I said, skeptically.

"That's actually very good," the nurse said. "That means that you might not have to have the tubes in for as long as seven to ten days. You may get them out sooner."

The nurses carefully helped me from the bed to the bathroom with my IV pole in tow. I made it in and sat down without much trouble at all. Then, out of nowhere, I felt a pang of nausea. And without thinking, I began reaching for the sick pan on the sink myself, as I was saying to the nurses, "I'm going to be sick."

Fortunately, I didn't do any damage in my stretch for the sick pan; and most importantly, 'I didn't come apart at the seams.'

I vomited twice more after that, just minutes after the nurses had put me back into bed, giving me a total of four sick episodes today. I was glad that my incision and drainage sites were still numb. But these episodes made me wonder what the anesthesiologist had put into my IV to 'prevent' me from getting sick. And immediately I found out. One of the nurses began telling me that two bags of Zofran had been added to my IV. Zofran was what they used for chemotherapy patients to help prevent or ease their nausea.

"So, you barreled through two bags of that," the nurse commented. "I'm going to let your anesthesiologist know how many times you've gotten sick so he can come by and check on you. He would want to know how sick you've been."

I thanked her as her shift was nearing its end.

As the evening sun set into nighttime, John hadn't left my side. I pleaded with him to go and grab some supper. He had to be starving, though he never confessed to it. I was actually developing an appetite myself, but I was on a Liquid Only Diet, which was fine with me.

When John finally conceded to go grab a bite in the hospital cafeteria, I fell back asleep for a while. *How much anesthesia is in me?* I started to wonder as I was awakening for the umpteenth time today.

As my eyes came into focus, John walked into the room alongside his brother, Jim, who had just gotten off from work and wanted to stop by and check on me and John. I knew of his possible coming ahead of time, because John had mentioned that he had received a call from Jim earlier in the downstairs lobby.

Jim's visit was very brief, of course, but the fact that he'd stopped by following a fourteen-hour workday was an act of incredible kindness that I will never forget.

It was almost midnight, and my sweet John was still with me. The nurses had told him that if he wanted to stay, to feel free to open the couch, as it unfolded into a pull-out bed. But I knew he would rest better at the hotel, which was only one minute away. I told him that I was just going to be sleeping, and I wanted him to be sleeping and resting well, too.

After much thought, John decided that he would go on back to the hotel. He stood up to kiss me, and then he took my left hand and said, "With this ring, I thee wed," as he slipped my wedding band back onto my finger.

Tears filled my eyes, and I couldn't speak past, "I love you so much, honey."

Those words meant everything on our wedding day back in 1997. But tonight, they meant even more.

15TH STOP *Slow (Fast) Moving Traffic*

I WOKE UP LOOKING into the face of Dublin, the stuffed dog, lying in the hospital bed next to me. I smiled at him, as he smiled back. Dublin's presence meant that John was already in the hospital somewhere, and I had slept through both of their arrivals. It was 8:15 a.m.; John hadn't left the hospital until a little after midnight last night, so he had either not slept long or returned to the hospital just hours after he'd gone. I found out that the latter was the case.

John entered my room just minutes after I awoke, kissed me, and told me that I had been sleeping so well and he hoped that he hadn't disturbed me upon his return to the hospital.

"Honey, what time did you get here?" I asked.

"Around six o'clock," he answered.

"Six? Honey, you didn't sleep much then," I said, concerned.

"I couldn't really sleep," he replied, softly. "When I got back to the hotel, I laid in bed and watched T.V. for a while. Then, I drifted off some. But I kept watching the clock, because I wanted to get back over here early to see how you were and how your night had been. You looked like you were resting well. Did you sleep during the night?"

"I slept some of it. I started feeling some pain around 4:30 this morning and asked the nurse if she would give me 'just a drop' of morphine. That's probably why I was sleeping so soundly and didn't know that you were here. Until I woke up and noticed Dublin in the bed with me, that is," I said, laughing.

The nurses had been asking me since early last evening if I needed any morphine, and not being a fan of that drug, because for me, it mimics anesthesia, I declined on their numerous offers. They told me that even if I wasn't in pain yet, the morphine would help stay ahead of the pain. But it wasn't until the early morning, when my eyes fluttered open for just a moment, that I felt the pain beginning to make its appearance. When I buzzed for the nurse, I requested that only a single drop of morphine be put into the IV, but I fell back asleep before it was administered. But I wasn't in pain right now, and I hadn't slept as long as morphine can keep me under, so I believed that the nurse had respected my dosage wishes.

I kissed John's hand that was wrapped around mine as a plate of scrambled eggs, escorted by a happy nurse, entered the room. This nurse reminded me of Amy, the Recovery Room nurse, whose joyful spirit had lifted and comforted me so greatly during my seconds of consciousness, though I had slept through most of her merriment.

I was hungry—another indication that I had received just a small amount of morphine. But as I reached for my fork, excruciating pain shot across my chest, and I could feel the incision and its dangling counterparts of drainage tubes for the very first time. This movement to grab for my fork instantly froze and debilitated me. I searched for a comfortable reclining position on the automatic bed with the knuckle of a finger that just happened to be closest to the controls.

John helped me to reposition and settle, and then he picked up the fork and started feeding me the eggs. I really hoped that this wasn't going to become a habit in the healing process—my sweetheart's hand spoon-feeding me.

Since it was possible that I was going to be discharged later today and sent off with Percocet for the pain, the nurse had me go ahead and swallow one following breakfast to calm my current agony. It took only minutes to set in, but the real effects of Percocet were still unknown to me. I was just glad for the absence, or numbness, of pain now.

About thirty minutes later, while I laid resting pain-free and still awake, one of the nurses came in to ask me if I felt like 'walking the length of the circular hall.' I was more than willing, as I oddly felt like I wanted to walk, anyway. (The nurses had asked me if I could try to walk some of the hall last night, and I astonishingly made it halfway down, not to the credit of my own ability.) John's eyes were as huge as my breakfast plate from this morning when the staff had asked me last night to do such a thing. But now, his eyes were as big as the tray that held the plate at the idea of my walking the *whole* hall this morning.

In his nervousness, John spoke up, saying, "Sweetie, I don't know if you should try that right now." He looked at the suggesting nurse, "I don't know if that's a good idea for her to do that just yet," he commented, retracing his concern.

"But I think I can do it, honey, or at least, try it," I said, patting his hand. "I'm a Navy SEAL, remember?" I jest. "Oh, not really," I said to the nurse, quickly clarifying that statement before she believed it. "John's been saying that to me throughout this journey to remind me of the strength he thinks I possess."

"That is so sweet," the nurse replied. "Well, whatever you both feel comfortable with concerning the hall walk," she continued, kindly. "You can always wait and walk later. Dr. Salydar just wants you up a little when you feel you are able."

I looked at John, reassuringly. "I'm okay to try it now," I said, not knowing if I would want to do it later, or if I would be awake to.

"Are you sure, sweetie?" John asked, with worried eyes.

"I'm sure with you by my side," I replied, which was my feeling as John's wife on a daily basis.

"Okay," John agreed. "But, go slow. Don't push yourself." he reminded.

I nodded in agreement.

When two more nurses showed up to help me out of bed, I first used the bathroom, and then, was ready to hit the hallway trail. But I unintentionally broke my promise to John soon out of the room about going slow as my pace began to nearly match my walking pace at school. I wasn't trying to mirror that. I didn't need to. But there was a boost of energy and stride in my step that wasn't from me. This strength was indescribable.

I had walked the hall's full long circle, down and around again, before I returned to bed. I wasn't even a little bit winded as I laid my head back on the pillow. I think the nurses were even speechless, as they left the room quite puzzled.

"Are you okay?" John asked, leaning over me.

"I really am," I commented.

John poured me some cold water, and as I sipped it from a straw, he contemplated over what had just happened. He sat down on the couch by my bed and said, "I can't believe you were able to walk the whole hall, twice. That was unbelievable." Then, as he pondered the idea more, he continued, "You know what I think? I think this is why God had you walking all over the school's campus at your job this year. That's the only explanation. You've walked so fast everyday this year that your body is conditioned and accustomed to walking at a good pace."

"That makes sense!" I said, now fully understanding God's purpose for my sprinting schedule at school. "I've said to you all year long that God was 'running me like I was in training for a marathon.' So, THIS is the marathon He was training me for!"

This sudden realization overwhelmed me as tears of guilt and thankfulness flowed down my cheeks, drenching my face and neck.

John got up to dry me off. "Honey, you're ingenious to have thought of that," I said.

"No," he corrected me. "God is ingenious to have thought of that."

"Yes, He is," I wholly agreed.

God had strengthened and prepared my body deliberately through my daily walk at school, for this walk. He had placed the physical energy and desire within me to want and be able to walk a far distance—walking this lengthy circled hall. That should have been more challenging, more difficult for me. But I didn't see or feel it as a difficult challenge at all. And, here's the real proof power of God: I walked a long way, pushing my IV pole alongside me with little assistance from the nurse or John, yet I couldn't even get out of the hospital bed without having lots of assistance.

Now that you know about this amazing plan of God's, I thought to myself, *use it wisely. Don't always be on 'blinking green.' A 'cautioned yellow light will surely appear,' so let yourself slow down, because God has equipped you for this walk.*

16TH STOP *Long Tunnel Ahead*

D R. SALYDAR CAME in to see me after lunch, though I don't remember much about lunch. The Percocet I had taken following breakfast had eventually knocked me out, and my hike around the hallway probably helped to precipitate that.

It was so great to see Dr. Salydar, as I hadn't seen her since I was in recovery, so I, of course, had some questions for her. The first question after she sat on my bed and wrapped her arms around me, though I couldn't reciprocate the hug because my arms couldn't do the extension, was, "Dr. Salydar, am I cancer-free?"

While I was fully awake for the answer now, I was nervous about her response.

"None of us are cancer-free. But I'll tell you this," Dr. Salydar remarked, "when you leave this world it won't be because of breast cancer."

"Oh, that's great!" I peeped out, with much relief.

"I only had to take one lymph node," Dr. Salydar continued. "The dye injection you had the other day lit it right up for me. That light was the passageway toward the cancer, and it highlighted the sentinel node—the only lymph node that showed it could have been compromised. I froze it and sliced it in surgery after I removed it, and I didn't find a trace of any cells in it. But I sent it off for a second opinion, just to be sure."

The 'second opinion' didn't surprise me at all, as Dr. Salydar always sent everything that she did 'off for a second opinion.' She liked having another set of eyes examine things.

Forgetting all my other questions after receiving the news that I wouldn't be leaving the world from breast cancer, I looked at John and asked if he had any questions. He did.

He looked at Dr. Salydar and asked, "So, how do you think the surgery and everything, overall, went?"

Oh yeah, that was one of the questions I was going to ask, I gestured to myself.

"Everything went really well," Dr. Salydar replied. "I got the cancer, but I did have to take more skin than I thought, so you'll feel some tightness for a while," she said, now looking at me. "I should have the surgery stage report within the next week. This report will identify the precise stage the cancer was in, which I anticipate to be no more than a Stage Two status. That report will also have the results of the second opinion I've requested on whether or not traces of cell findings are discovered in the removed lymph node. Terrie, you did so well in surgery," Dr. Salydar said, smiling proudly at me.

So, that's what I did well, I thought, remembering Amy's words to me in recovery. *I wonder how you do well at something, though, when you're sound asleep?* I contemplated.

"Let me check your incision," Dr. Salydar said, peeking down into my gown. "That looks good," she commented. "So, how are you feeling?"

"I've begun to have a little pain and had a small amount of morphine at 4:30 this morning, and a Percocet after breakfast," I said.

I told Dr. Salydar about the shooting pain that had traveled across my chest when I reached for my breakfast fork.

"You aren't going to have your reach back for a while as your incision is healing," Dr. Salydar replied. "Any sudden movement or jerk will instigate pain, just for the first couple of weeks. You won't be able to lie flat down in the bed. You'll need to sit propped up with pillows, because you'll feel your incision pulling and be in a lot of pain if you are flat. And, I don't want you to extend your arms above your shoulder level at all, as that will cause you great pain, too. I'll be putting you with a physical therapist in a few weeks to work with you on getting your reach back, helping you with wound care, and lymphedema prevention."

Listening to all of this about the surgery stage report still to come, along with my pain and limitations that were already here, ushered in some concern, thus taking over the joyful corner inside me. While the surgery had gone well, all the information mixed in the bowl together with it, didn't sound like I was completely out of the woods yet.

Trying to push out my worries, I announced to Dr. Salydar, "Did the nurses tell you that I walked the whole hall this morning and half last night?"

"Yes!" Dr. Salydar screamed. "That's amazing! And, listen, I'm going to send you out of here, back to the hotel, this afternoon. I want you to take Percocet for the pain. But, if the Percocet doesn't work well with you, because it does have some strong side effects, switch to Ibuprofen—taking about three of those at a time to stay ahead of the pain."

She hugged John and me before she left to make the discharge arrangements, telling us to call her if I had any problems at all.

My sweet John was going to be draining the four drainage tubes that hung acrobatically from my chest. He was given a chart to record the level of fluid drained from each pouched tube. He would be draining all four every twelve hours. Once the level, from even one tube, was less than 25cc in a 24-hour period, I could have that drain removed. Pam, Dr. Salydar's nurse, had told John that he would need to call her every morning at nine o'clock with the daily readings, and if one was below the required level, she would have John bring me to the office that day and have that tube taken out. So, John and I may make four different trips across the mountain, depending upon when each tube equalized and remained at the desired output level.

One of the nurses came in and trained John on the draining procedures of each tube. Thankfully, my gown remained covering my chest area so that only the tubes were exposed for John to view. But, for the first time, I felt a throb of pain as the nurse was draining the pouched tubes, one at a time, especially from the ones on the left side of me. I could feel pressure and coldness at the apparent sites. I was hoping that was just a fluke incident. Maybe she was draining them slower in order to teach John. *That's gotta be it,* I thought.

Another nurse entered, ready to help me out of bed and get me changed into the sweater and gaucho pants I'd worn in the morning of my surgery. John sat on the couch with the repacked bag I'd brought for my hospital stay.

I kept my eyes fixed toward the ceiling as the nurse began peeling off my gown. I glanced over at John, for just a second, and that was the very moment he was seeing my new body for the first time, as his face fell frozen and expressionless at the sight. I immediately turned my head in the opposite direction, now staring up at the other side of the ceiling.

I wanted to ask John if he were okay. I wanted to hold him. I wanted to ask him what I looked like. But I kept my head turned as my eyes filled with tears, wanting to console him and wondering what the unimaginable sight of me was, at the same time. I didn't want him to see my tears, so once the nurse had gotten my sweater on me, I brought my eyes to its sleeve and wiped away the evidence.

As the nurse finished putting on my shoes, I went over and sat in the chair beside John. He was watching another nurse sort some papers on my bed.

"Are you okay, sweetheart?" I asked him, as I rubbed on his hand.

"Yeah, I'm fine," he said, nervously. "Are you okay? Did it hurt for them to change you?"

"I could feel it some, but I'm fine," I said. "That's kind of crazy that I can't pull up my own gaucho pants, huh? I mean, c'mon," I joked, in an effort to shrink the incomprehensible giant in the room.

"I'll help you with all that, sweetie," John said, now reaching for my hand. "Remember you can't do any sudden movements or jerks. And, we don't need your drainage tubes or incision areas to become irritated and compromised, or worse, become too painful for you."

"Thanks honey," I said, locking my tears inside me.

Before we left the hospital, John made arrangements with the staff to borrow a wheelchair so he could get me up to our hotel room. They kindly agreed and asked that he just return it to the downstairs front lobby once he got me settled in the room.

John reached for my flower pillow that I'd kept in the car to protect my chest area from the strain and pressure of the seatbelt.

I felt so weak, almost faint, as John helped me from the car to the wheelchair at the hotel's entrance. But, thankfully, that feeling didn't hang around long.

John got me in the room with no problem and helped me sit in a big chair near the window where I had a wide view to the outside world. He turned on the television and said he'd be right back, as he left to return the borrowed wheelchair.

I looked around the room as the hotel door closed behind John, thinking to myself, *it's over, and I made it. I'm back at the hotel, and now, all I need to do is rest and recover.* I began thanking and praising God for carrying me through the surgery, because I knew that He was the reason I'd gotten through it. He was the Great Physician!

John wasn't gone long when the faint feeling began creeping back up on me. And this time, it brought nausea along with it. I started to get myself up from the chair and quickly realized that I couldn't. I couldn't even budge. Even the slightest movement awakened my incision and tube sites, and I was suddenly paralyzed by the pain that my small attempt to relocate myself had provoked. Just then, I heard a key in the door, and as it opened, John appeared. He immediately fled toward me, sensing something was wrong.

"Honey, I don't feel too good," I told him, as he reached me. "I'm sick to my stomach, and I feel like I might pass out. I tried to get up and go to the bed, but I can't move. I tried, but I think my pain medicine is wearing off, because I'm in some pain," I said, almost collapsing into John at this point.

"I got you, sweetie," he said, as he slowly got me up from the chair and laid me on the bed. He propped up several pillows behind me since Dr. Salydar had said for me not to lie flat down. John then reached for the bottle of Percocet.

"I think you should take another one of these, if you can," John said. "You haven't had one since this morning, and they want you to 'stay ahead of the pain.' Do you think you can get one down, sweetie?"

"I think so," I replied inside my spinning head.

Just seconds after I swallowed the Percocet, I fell asleep, or passed out. And, I didn't wake up until sometime in the night when I noticed John sitting up on his elbow next to my face, watching me. I tried to speak, but I just smiled, falling back into my sleeping abyss.

When I awoke fully the next morning, John was already up and showered and making some coffee.

"Hey, honey," I said.

"Hey, sweetie," he said back, as he walked over to my side of the bed.

"How are you feeling?" he asked, concerned.

"I'm fine, I think. Honey, I saw you watching me last night. Please tell me that you slept some," I pleaded.

"I didn't sleep much," John replied. "I wanted to make sure that you were okay and keep a check on you, so I watched you most of the night."

"Oh, honey," I said, with love and worry in my voice. "You have to sleep. I'm fine. I'll wake you if I need something, but I want you to get some rest."

"We'll see," he said, smiling and rubbing his hand across my forehead.

"I think I'm going to try to go to the bathroom, honey," I announced.

"Well, let me help you," John replied.

I couldn't get up by myself again. Not at all. John came close into me, uncovered my legs to carefully move them out from beneath the blanketed sheets, took my hands into his, and gently turned and lifted me from the bed. Then he wrapped one of his arms quickly around me. I couldn't stand straight up this morning. The weighty pain of the pouched tubes was pulling me down so that I was slightly hunchbacked.

John sat me down once we reached the bathroom, disrobing my bottom half, which I also was unable to manipulate. He stepped out and said he'd be right outside the door when I was done. I was done fast. As my stomach churned with nausea, I stared at the trash can beneath the sink that I couldn't reach, and the bathroom began to turn black. I yelled for John, telling him that I was going to pass out. I felt him scoop me up into his arms and carry me back to the bed. I went unconscious for a moment and awoke trying to catch my breath. John stood beside me with my hand in his.

"I'm sorry, honey," I said, looking up at him and truly feeling sorry for what he had endured with me already in the short time we had returned to the hotel.

"It's okay, sweetie," he said, as his eyes and words became suddenly flooded with tears.

John turned as he began to break down. I desperately wanted to wrap my arms around him, but I could only hold his hand, which I rubbed inside of mine, as I said, "Honey, it's going to be okay. I'm okay, and we're going to get through this. Sweetheart, I don't want you to worry. Everything is going to be fine."

Not being able to speak back, John walked over to the microwave. And still broken up, he began making me breakfast.

It was then that I realized, this wasn't just *my* journey; it was *our* journey. John had been just as affected with emotional layers peeled from him as they had been from me. And now, he was the indefinite caregiver of a newly landscaped wife with definite needs and uncertain outcomes.

17ᵀᴴ STOP *Left Shoulder Closed—Merge Right*

J OHN AND I made an 'executive decision' after breakfast that I would stop taking the Percocet. The side effects from that drug were about as bad as my pain spells. It was time to switch to Ibuprofen. But that switch was going to have to wait as my stomach continued to rumble, threatening to reject just two small spoonfuls of oatmeal.

It was late morning when the oatmeal finally calmed in the restless sea of my stomach. I still had on the clothes that I had entered and left the hospital in, and they were warm and comfortable enough for me to keep on. But John thought it was time for a fresh change in the form of pajamas. Reluctantly, I agreed, because John was going to see my new body again. And this time, it was going to be up close.

As he took my hands and gently lifted me up to a sitting position on the side of the bed and began unbuttoning my sweater, I commented, in an attempt to lighten the moment, "Man, I hope my deodorant is still holding out from Thursday or this is going to be really bad for you."

John laughed, now face to face with my bare torso, though not seeming to be too affected by the view this time. Or pretending not to be.

"Sweetie, I don't smell a thing, so I think you're okay," he replied, as he continued to unclothe my sweater from me.

"Actually," he continued, "I don't think you'll be able to wear deodorant for a while, because it could get into your incision."

I gasped at the thought. And then, I remembered. "Honey, you're right," I confirmed. "One of the papers I got from Dr. Salydar's nurse stated that 'deodorant can't be applied for seven to ten days after surgery.' Double rats!" I said, looking at John's sweet face as he smiled and shook his head.

"You'll be fine, sweetie," he said, assuredly.

After John got me into my pajamas, he helped me to the bathroom where I sat down as he washed my face with a warm, soapy cloth. This was the beginning of several more sponge baths that John happily, and without hesitation or thought, would give me.

My friend and hairdresser, Peggy, had told me about a no-rinse shampoo that is poured onto dry hair, lathered in, and towel-dried, giving the look, feel and smell of clean, shampooed hair without the use of water. So, after John and I left the bathroom, he sat me down in a desk chair that faced a mirror, as he welcomed me to "John's Salon."

He pulled out the bottle of No-Rinse and wrapped a bath towel around my neck for a drape. Mimicking a conversation that Peggy and I would have in her salon, John commented as he massaged the shampoo into my hair, "So, how's your mom? She was all upset when she came in the other day about the road construction going on near her apartment."

I laughed and laughed as John stayed in the character of Peggy during most of the shampooing session, which would also become the first of many that he did for me.

When John was done, I asked as I do of Peggy, "How much do I owe you?"

"This one's on the house," John said, removing the bath towel from around my neck. "For you, John's Salon is always on the house, where we're happy to treat our repeat customers."

We both laughed as he began brushing my hair. As I looked at John's kind face in the mirror, I said, "Honey, I do owe you; it will just never be payment enough. You are my greatest gift from God, and you have my heart and all my love. I'm so grateful for you and to you, and I'll never be able to thank you enough for all you are to me and all you do for me."

John looked at me lovingly and replied, "You don't have to thank me, sweetie. This is part of the deal. This is what I'm here for. 'In sickness and in health,' remember?"

"I remember, sweetheart. I remember every word inside of every vow that we said to each other. And if these shoes were on your feet instead of mine, you would have all of my care, too," I said.

John kissed me on top of my clean head. "I know I would," he remarked.

I felt so clean and refreshed from my sponge bath and shampoo. But I also felt oddly tired, though I had done nothing except move from the bed to the bathroom to the desk chair, all in slow motion and half bent over as the drainage tubes continued to pose me downward toward the floor.

I sat up for just a short while before needing to lie back down in the bed following my appointments with John. As I rested, John made us some sandwiches for lunch. And my dessert would be the first round of three Ibuprofen tablets, which I was about ready for, as I could feel inklings of pain stirring here and there amongst the drainage sites.

As John ate his sandwich from a comfy chair and I from the bed, my curiosity of my new body arose, and I just had to ask the question that had been burning within me since yesterday when John had his first look at me, and his full panorama today. "Honey, what do I look like?" I asked, softly.

John didn't seem ready for that question this early on, but he must have anticipated it at some point, because his answer back to me rolled out like a rehearsed response. "Sweetie, you had major surgery, and you're going to heal from it, but you don't need to look at it anytime soon. I would wait for about six weeks, because when it heals, it's going to look better," he said, trying to convince one, or both, of us that that was true.

I didn't want to push the issue or make John anymore uncomfortable than that question, assuredly, already had. So, I simply concurred with his reply.

"Six weeks sounds good to me," I complied. "I can definitely wait that long, because I'm in no hurry to see myself." (Neither John nor I, at the time, thought about my needing a real shower or bath before then. Regardless, if one of us had thought of it, we both believed that my waiting six weeks was a good and solid plan.)

As time moved along during my hotel recovery stay, after numerous naps and periodic walks down to the lobby and across the front sidewalk, my body began responding to movement. But not in the way that John or I had expected it would.

Once I would return to a lying down position following any upright activity, pain from the drainage tubes quickly evolved into a roaring lion with sharp, piercing bites. And even though I had taken six Ibuprofen pills in the last eight hours, the drainage tubes were awakening from their numbing sleep, leaving the Ibuprofen as no match for this fierce cat.

Tears filled my eyes each time John, apologetically, had to drain the tubes, as the pressure of releasing the fluid escalated the pain into excruciating levels. I could no longer bear my left arm resting against my body without a buffer between the two. So, John brought me a folded hand towel that I placed beneath my arm and upon the left side drainage areas so that something soft and thick could, hopefully, calm and cushion them.

I had earlier thought that the four anesthetized drainage tubes that hung from me would turn out to be around the same weight as my real breasts had been. Though apparently, the precarious placements of the tubes and their pouches, along with their unexpected heaviness, were my challenges in keeping an upright position; hence, my walking bent over. They had, in all aspects, become like pendulum weights, giving way to the perpetual chains that bound them.

The compilation of drugs, though, had still kept me from experiencing any pain from my incision area, which I was grateful for. But on this second night as John drained all four tubes once again, for the first time in my adult life, I wanted my breasts back. I laid saturated in my own tears wanting desperately to change my mind on something that I could never undo.

On Sunday, our last day and night at the hotel before heading back home, the pain from the two left-side drainage localities had put the left portion of my body into a debilitative state, whereby I could no longer move my left shoulder, arm or fingers. The slightest motion would set the drainage sites into immediate distress. And I couldn't lie down, sit up, stand, walk, sit down, or move without assistance from John. We even developed a count system, whereby we would both count to three, and on three, John would move me. Sometimes, we would do what I called "a soft three," which meant that I needed to move very slowly and carefully from the spot that I was in.

I now couldn't be without the hand towel for a second, even in my sleep, that laid tucked between my left arm and left drainage points.

The Ibuprofen worked when it wanted to, or when the pain lessened enough to allow it in. And, during those moments when I would lay in bed, pain-free, and try to watch T.V., my thoughts and inward fears of the unknown ahead would carry me to a dark place that I couldn't turn from. There was no escape inside my head. Until I prayed to God about my fears. Then whenever my mind would be imparted to that darkness, God would be there with His broom to sweep the black dust into light. (God swept a lot in the weeks ahead.)

Around 9:30 p.m. on Sunday night, the pain became intolerable as John finished dumping the last tube. He apologized profusely, assuring me that he was almost done.

John slid a cool cloth across my perspiring forehead, kissing me, and asking what he could do. He was lying in the bed beside me, still fully dressed. I knew what I needed him to do. I needed him to take me over to the hospital. And, just as I opened my mouth to tell him, the exhaustion and burden from the pain caused me to succumb to a fainting, deep sleep.

I woke up sometime in the middle of the night. John was sound asleep, which I'd supposed was the first time he had slept since my surgery. He was fatigued even more than I, as he was constantly tending to me unless I was, myself, asleep. My pain had subsided, and I closed my eyes thanking God, as He drew me back into slumber.

God and John took incredible care of me in ways that I never imagined I would ever need taking care of in these days, or, in my life. Sometimes I felt as if I were on the outside of the hotel's building looking in through a wide fictional window, where I was the main character inside of an unbelievable, mythical dream.

God shields me from all the things that I can't protect or save myself from. And, John shields me from the cold, the heat, and the other elements in between. The Lord God is my Savior and my constant strength. And, John is the solid rock that God put into my life.

18TH STOP *Caution! This Vehicle Makes Wide Right Turns*

I WAS A LITTLE nervous about the drive home today. Not just because it was Memorial Day, quadrupling the traffic on the roads, but I didn't know how I would do riding in the car for an hour. John armed me with three Ibuprofen and asked the hotel, upon checkout, if I could leave with their hand towel that had become my *Linus blanket*, telling them to 'please charge us for it' if they permitted me to keep it. They not only insisted that I take it at no charge, but I overheard them offer John a second one for me to take as well at no cost. He declined on the offering of the second towel and sincerely thanked them for the one they were giving me. *How kind*, I thought, as I sat across from the checkout counter with their priceless gift pressed up against me. This towel would be the perfect companion to my flower pillow that rode between me and the seatbelt. And, once John had me 'locked and loaded' into the seat, I was amazingly comfortable.

God kept my pain at bay on the drive home, and John was careful and mindful of the roads with their bumps and curves, constantly checking with me on how I was. I don't know if it was just John's choosing or if it was the plentiful traffic around us, but he stayed in the right lane almost all the way home, taking his time among other cars that traveled as if they were running out of it.

I was happy to be home, but also anxious. My new body had gotten used to our hotel room—the higher and adjustable bed, the firmly padded chair with superior cushioning, a taller toilet, and, of course, the perfect chair for my shampoos at 'John's Salon.' That thought made me chuckle and helped me realize that God was certainly going to make me comfortable in my own home, with John by my side to help make it so, too.

Phone calls from our family started coming in shortly after our arrival back home. John and I had both spoken to them some during our hotel stay.

When lunch was over and the phone's ring settled, I grew very fatigued, so John helped me up from our not-so-comfortable couch (that was uncomfortable before my surgery) and into our bed that already had a pile of propped-up pillows awaiting me.

"What can I get for you, sweetie?" John asked, sweeping my hair to the side of my face with his fingers.

"I'm good, honey. I'm just going to rest a while, and I hope you can, too. Thanks for everything, sweetheart," I said to the man of my dreams from the woman of his current calamity.

"Well, I'm going to start on the laundry," my dream man replied. "I'll keep the door open so I can hear you if you need anything, and I'll be checking on you, too."

"Sleep somewhere in between, my love," I pleaded. "I know you've got to be worn out."

"I will," John said, "in between laundry loads." He kissed me and headed toward the laundry room. I knew the only dirty laundry that we had was what we'd worn on our journey. I'd washed everything in the hamper, including the towels and bed linens prior to our leaving, so I hoped that the laundry was as small a load as I was laying there picturing.

The bed was quite comfortable, and it didn't take long before I drifted off to sleep. Though, I was very warm, and the bedroom very humid, when I awoke after sleeping for almost three hours. I called for John only once, and then heard him on the phone. This call didn't sound like a family call. This was business.

"Are there other homes in the subdivision without power?" I heard him ask.

I looked over at the clock on the nightstand, flashing 4:57 p.m. *Ugh, our power's out,* I realized. *My poor sweetheart. He doesn't need this, too,* I thought, sighing to myself.

John hung up and came into the bedroom. "The power's out," he announced. "But, it's only our house that Dominion knows of, for now."

"That doesn't sound good," I commented. "How can it just be our house?"

"It could be a breaker somewhere. They're sending someone out to look around. Sweetie, if you feel like getting up, you'll be cooler out front in the living room," John said. "It's too hot for you to stay in here."

He was right, and my perspiring wasn't going to help my deodorant situation, or should I say, my non-deodorant situation.

"Yeah, I'll go back to the couch, honey," I replied.

"On three, then," John said, as we began our unison counting.

While the couch wasn't as comfortable and kind to my body as the bed was, it was definitely cooler, so I wasn't about to complain. Plus, the Ibuprofen had worked well managing my pain today, so I had nothing to complain about even if I wanted to. I was flat-out blessed, and God was going to get us through this power outage just like He had gotten us through the beginning of this expedition.

When Dominion Electric pulled up outside, John went out to meet them. He was surprised to also find our next-door neighbor awaiting their arrival. She had come over to our yard to meet John and Dominion. As it turned out, our neighbor was also without power. And, as the men from Dominion began their research, they discovered that the problem was underground in a wire that shared power between the two residences.

More men were called in on the job, as this was going to require hours that went into the overnight. The men were able to turn the power back on, but only for a short time, as there could be no active current running when they began to dig up the side yard between our homes, and later, to replace the wire that had completely deteriorated.

One of the men rang the doorbell around 8:45 p.m. and told John that he was going to have to cut the power off for good in fifteen more minutes. John closed the door behind him and scurried over to me. "We have to drain your tubes now, sweetie," he said, hurriedly. "We only have fifteen minutes before Dominion cuts the power back off, and I don't think it would be a good idea to drain your tubes by flashlight."

"Oh, I agree," I said nervously at the thought.

John had been draining the tubes in the twelve-hour cycles of 9 a.m. and 9 p.m. His first call to Dr. Salydar's nurse had been this morning at nine o'clock to inform her of the levels and to alert her of the pain that the tubes on my left side were causing. Nurse Pam thought that the levels on the left-side tubes may be low enough to remove tomorrow, but she couldn't 'guarantee that possibility, as it might be too soon to start removing any tubes.'

I sat on the couch as John prepared to drain the first of four tubes. He worked carefully and a bit more quickly than he had had to before, because we were, literally, nearing 'lights out.' John recorded the numbers on the chart as he moved along from tube to tube, just as he had been doing.

As he began to drain from the left-side tubes, the pain that had remained silenced for several hours awoke in a violent fury. Maybe it was because I was sitting up for the first time as the tubes were drained. Maybe it was because we were hurrying. Nonetheless, I immediately buried my face into my right hand and quietly sobbed, trying with everything in me not to rattle or startle John. But he wasn't blind. He spoke and reacted instantly to my body beginning to now lean toward the right as if to pull itself away from the agonizing pain.

"Sweetie, I'm almost done. Try to stay upright so the tube doesn't slip out. Hang in there. We're almost through," John said, slightly panicking himself now.

I couldn't speak. I was afraid to speak, so I just nodded. In my mind, speaking would have been interpreted by the tubes as me talking back to them. I didn't see these tubes as objects anymore. I imagined them as belonging to an octopus, with its huge head trapped inside of me, while its arms swung from my outside. And, each time one of its arms on the left side was squeezed by John, it retaliated, thrashing and gouging me in warful defense.

In the next instant, John was finished. The draining of the tubes was over. But the attack of the angry octopus kept my body motionless for several moments, leaving me still leaning toward the right side of the couch.

"Okay, sweetie, just sit still and catch your breath a minute. I'll be right back," John said, as he collected the charts with the readings and took them back to his desk. He got distracted for just a moment as he glanced out the window to see what the men were doing now.

He returned to me. "Sweetie, do you want to go to the bathroom? I think we still have a few minutes, and we'll take a flashlight, just in case. What do you think? Do you want to try to go?"

"Yes, I'll try," I said, regaining slow movement.

John guided me up from the couch on three-count and took me into the bathroom, as my body continued to lean to the right. Just as he helped me up from going, the doorbell rang. "You go on, honey," I said. "I'm just going to wash and rinse my right hand under the water, so I'll be fine."

"I'll be right back," John said, running to the front door.

My left arm was now positioned against me like it was in a sling. I couldn't move it at all, the hand towel from the hotel still anchored between it and my body. When I went to dry my right hand on the hanging towel, I slightly moved the index finger on my left hand to lift the towel's corner. The pain of the drainage tubes quaked me so hard that I cried out. John came running. I laid my head on his shoulder unable to take anymore. My body was bent and mangled, protruding toward the right and not wanting to be alive, or awake, for any further pain.

John gave me three Ibuprofen and laid me in the extra bedroom bed where it was cooler, just before the lights went totally out. John laid down in the bed beside me. The window beside us was lit only by the huge work light outside that hung above the unearthed hole.

I didn't last long in the extra bed. Its mattress was firmer than ours, and it was keeping me, and the octopus, wide awake.

"Honey," I whispered. "I think I'm going to have to sleep in our bed. This bed's too firm. I'm so sorry," I said, completely hating to disturb John anymore.

In his quick wit, I was waiting for him to call me Goldilocks following my comment about this bed being too hard. But, in his weariness, that thought never surfaced for him.

"Let's sleep in our own bed. Actually, I think we'll both sleep better there, because this light and the drilling that will come about soon will keep us up, anyway," John remarked.

So, on three, with my body making wide right turns as John navigated me and the flashlight toward our bedroom, we reached the foot of our bed. Amidst the thick humid air, I was cold and craving the warmth of covers around me and my hand towel. I don't remember much after John put me in the bed, other than closing my eyes.

I awoke, for just a moment, sometime in the early morning hours and noticed the lit lantern on our dresser as coolness encompassed the room. The power was back on. I could hear my sweet John sleeping on the couch. It was the best sound I had heard in days. *We are absolutely in God's hands,* I thought. *And He holds all the power.*

19ᵀᴴ STOP *Uneven Lanes*

I T WAS TUESDAY, May 27, 2014, and I didn't know it yet, but today was going to be a good day. Though, it didn't start out that way.

John and my morning began as it had for the past three mornings—breakfast at 8:30 a.m., squeezing the arms of the octopus at 9:00 a.m., and me in my tear-stained pajama top by 9:15 a.m. from the left-side drainings.

John made his morning call to Dr. Salydar's nurse with this morning's new levels. I wasn't sure how much longer I was going to be able to handle these drainage tubes and the induced pain that they provoked. And, when John hung up with the nurse, I found out that I wasn't going to have to deal with them much longer at all. Based on the new readings, three out of four of the tubes had fallen and remained below the 25cc requirement.

"Nurse Pam said that three of the tubes can be taken out today," John happily declared as he returned to the bedroom. "And, two of the three are the ones on your left side. They are both coming out with one on the right."

Tears of elation poured from my eyes. "What? Honey, are you serious? I can't believe it! They're removing three of them?"

"They are," John confirmed. "Nurse Pam is going to call me back to let me know what time we can come this afternoon."

And then it hit me. "So, you don't have to drain those three anymore?" I asked, thoroughly steeped in my salt-water tears now.

John hugged me as I laid my head against him. "No, sweetie," he replied, softly. "We are totally done with draining those. I told Nurse Pam how much pain you've been in and how it has practically prohibited the left side of your upper body from any movement. That really concerned her, so I'm wondering if they would've removed the left tubes anyway, regardless of the levels."

Still leaning my head on John's stomach, something occurred to me. I asked with a muffled voice from my face being pressed into him, "Honey, did you fudge the numbers a little bit, Dr. Childress?"

"No, sweetie," John said, laughing. "I really didn't. But I thought about it. I couldn't stand to keep seeing you in that kind of pain. I felt so responsible because . . . "

I interrupted. "Honey, you weren't responsible for my pain. You didn't have a choice but to drain the tubes. You were just doing what you had been told," I proclaimed. "But I thought you might be feeling that way. It wasn't your fault, and you were always so careful and gentle. You drained them perfectly and efficiently, every time. I don't think too many people could have done that with the painful state I went into. But, look at you," I said, now smiling up at his face, "my Navy SEAL medic."

John smiled back at me. "I'm just glad they're coming out."

"And now, you'll only need to drain the one tube. That won't take near as long, and I don't feel any pain on the right side when you're draining."

Unbeknownst to me at the time, I would eat those words later, unless the one-armed octopus still left dangling from me, swallowed me up first.

John went to get our golden retriever, Biscuit, later in the morning from the kennel where he'd been staying during our time away. I couldn't wait to see him, and it would give me normalcy and routine to have Biscuit back home with us.

My body, still incapacitated from the left tubes, remained bent over when I went to greet him as he walked in the front door with John. Biscuit watched me move about with a puzzled look on his face. He probably found it odd that our noses were nearly parallel. And talk about looking each other right in the eye! This quickly concerned Biscuit and caused his worry to develop into a sympathy limp for me, whereby he only walked on three legs.

"Biscuit, Mommy's not limping," I would say. "Why are *you* limping?"

John snuck up behind me pretending to talk as he thought Biscuit might sound if he could speak. "Mommy, I'm limping because I can't get any lower to the floor than I already am to be bent like you. So, when you can walk right again, I'll walk right again."

I laughed and cried, both at once, at what John (and Biscuit) had said. It was so endearing, and Biscuit limped the rest of the day as I walked bent over.

Nurse Pam called back with a 3:30 p.m. appointment to have the three tubes removed. We got there around 3:00 p.m., in the hopeful event that the tubes could come out even a few minutes earlier. My name was called at 3:15 p.m., as my bent body and John's upright one met Nurse Pam at the door.

"Terrie, bless your heart," Nurse Pam said. "John said you were in a lot of pain, and this is definitely not a good body position for you."

"These tubes have been something else, Pam," I replied. "I never would have imagined pain like this. My incision hasn't seemed to bother me at all, unless of course, its pain has simply been masked by the trumpeting pain of these drainage tubes."

"Well," Nurse Pam commented, "we're going to take care of getting those out of you right now."

Nurse Pam was prepping a tray with bandages and square gauze. "What I'm going to have you do as I remove each one . . ."

"Oh," I interrupted. "I thought Dr. Salydar was going to remove them."

"No, this is the part that I do. But you will be seeing her next week for your scheduled appointment. For us to be able to remove the tubes the same day once they've fallen and stayed below 25cc, Dr. Salydar would have to take walk-ins, and she just can't do that with her surgery schedules. So, I take care of drainage tube removals. I promise I'm gentle. I've been doing this for quite a long time," Nurse Pam reassured me.

I trusted Nurse Pam, but I didn't trust how I was going to get through being awake for this removal procedure, so I asked (begged) her, "Is there any way that you can sedate me or numb the sites before you remove them? Hey, you can even sock me in the face to knock me out if you want," I remarked, my face now hit by abounding tears.

"Terrie, I'm sorry. We don't numb or sedate you for this. There's actually a breathing exercise that I'm going to have you do as each tube is removed. This exercise helps you not to feel much, and the tube comes out with one quick pull," Nurse Pam explained.

"Okay," I sighed. I looked up at John who had his arm around me. *I can't believe I have to breathe during this*, I thought to myself, and then realized how illogical that thought was.

We practiced. Nurse Pam had me repeat the breathing

exercise after her several times. It was an easy exercise, but the anticipated pain that I suspected I would be in continued to cloud the ease of it all. I was to take in a deep breath and then blow it out hard as if blowing out several lit candles atop a cake.

John and Nurse Pam both helped me climb up and lay down on the cushioned bed table. Nurse Pam removed my *Linus blanket* hand towel that I still had pressed up against the left side of me. John took my hand, as I 'held on for dear life' to his. Having something removed from a woman's body after Lamaze-like breathing is commonly known as childbirth. But I was having limbs of an octopus removed from mine. And, never having experienced childbirth, myself, I was unable to discern between the worst pain of the two. As I lay there trying.

It was time to breathe in, as Nurse Pam positioned her hand at the first left tube entrance. After taking air in, I blew out like I was extinguishing a thousand candles. I felt that one slightly, but I knew the next tube on the left to be pulled had been the main culprit of my pain.

"Breathe in," Nurse Pam instructed, and then she pulled. I stopped breathing; I mean, blowing out. I laid there motionless, speechless, and emotional as tears filled my eyes and lined my cheeks.

"Why are you crying?" Nurse Pam asked, concerned.

"It hurt, but I'm fine. And I think I'm just relieved that those two are finally out of me," I responded, winded from the pain, or from blowing out all those candles. Or, from not breathing for a few seconds.

"Terrie, that tube was up around your rib cage bones. I don't know if it was just resting there or entangled, but that tube was right up against your rib cage. And that's why I think you were in so much pain," Nurse Pam announced.

"That would also cause your body to bend over, as you were, to compensate for and try to override the pain."

"So, that's what was going on," John remarked. "I wondered about its location when I was draining that tube. I thought it looked too close to bones."

"Another reason could be," Nurse Pam went on, "that you're so thin up there, you may have been more sensitive to the feeling of that tube resting on your rib cage."

"Now, Pam," I jest, "are you just saying that I'm thin because you have one more tube to pull?"

Nurse Pam laughed. "No, I mean that. You are thin up here. And, yes, I do have one more tube to pull—on the right side. So hopefully, this one will go better for you. Breathe in."

Still squeezing John's hand, I breathed in, blew out, and felt nothing as Nurse Pam pulled at the right tube.

Three of the four tubes were out. I looked up at John, relieved. He leaned down and whispered, "See? You *are* strong. You *are* a warrior. You *are* a Navy SEAL."

"But I still want my hand towel back," I return whispered, needing it now to comfort the sore effects of the tubes' existence inside me.

We laughed as Nurse Pam bandaged the bleeding, tubeless holes. "Now, let's get you walking upright again," Nurse Pam said, as she and John helped me down from the bed and she led us out to the exit.

"I feel like I can already see more of the world in front of me," I commented, all of us laughing as John and I prepared to leave.

"I'll talk to you in the morning," John said to Nurse Pam as the door closed behind us.

When we returned home and I started working on getting my posture back, I felt uneven and unbalanced. I wasn't stumbling or unsure-footed; I just felt a bit angled.

I wondered if that was because of having only one tube and drainage pouch hanging from me now on the lower right side. Although, I had been cautioned earlier by Dr. Salydar that my balance may be off, somewhat, until my body adjusted to the absence of my breasts. *Maybe that's it,* I thought. But it didn't really matter. I was less three tubes, with one to go!

I kept walking my uneven lanes throughout the house, just glad to be tall again. And Biscuit, all of a sudden, was walking better, too.

20TH STOP *Unmarked Pavement Ahead*

A s JOHN DRAINED the one right tube remaining, it was easier and much more painless for both of us. Until a little over twenty-four hours had passed from when the other tubes had been withdrawn.

I began feeling some pain from this right-side tube late the evening of May 28th, though I hadn't mentioned it to John, as he had been through enough anguish of his own within this draining dungeon of me.

I never looked at the drainage tubes, as I'd only seen their connected pouches full of my juices contained inside them, so I didn't know how close *this* tube might be to my rib cage. And, I'd never felt pain from it before. John and I had been so excited over the removal of the other tubes, especially the left ones. I just couldn't bring myself to tell him that I was now experiencing pain from this one. So, the pain told him instead.

When John proceeded to drain the tube at nine o'clock the evening of the 28th, I began wincing, then softly weeping into my hand.

"Do you feel that?" John asked, surprised.

"Yes," was all I could say.

"Is this the first time you've felt it?" asked John.

I needed to answer him. I needed air to answer him. I started doing the breathing exercise that Nurse Pam had taught me. While that exercise provided me some calmness and a little extra breath, it definitely wasn't intended to take away existing pain.

"Honey," my mouth blew out, "I've been having some pain with this tube for a few hours. I was dreading you draining it tonight, because I thought I may feel it. But this is the first time I have felt it during the draining. It was fine this morning. I don't know why it's causing me pain. Is this one close to my rib cage like the left one was?"

"No," replied John, now breathless himself. "This one is actually to the right of your rib cage, so I don't think this tube is compromising anything."

I was still sore from the punctured holes of the removed tubes, and I still had the hand towel folded against the left side of me. John and I had guessed that there could be some internal bruising from the initial attack on my rib cage that was keeping that left pain stirring whenever I brought my body from a sitting to a standing position, and vice versa. So, with this new pain development, I was beginning to feel like I had all four tubes back inside of me. The octopus's arms that I had had vacated the day before had either left remnants of itself behind or had a twin residing that we didn't know about.

In an effort to erase the worried look that currently consumed John's face, I remarked, "Honey, you know what? I was able to get through, by God's mercy and your steady hands, the incredible pain of the two tubes on my left side. So, getting through just this one tube on my right is going to be doable for me. I'm not giving up my Navy ship yet, and I still need my captain, which is you. So, all aboard, my love!"

John smiled and kissed me. "I'm always going to be on board," he promised. "You know, your level on this tube is at 22cc tonight. If it stays at that level, maybe this tube can come out tomorrow or the day after, then you could have it out before the weekend."

"Are we fudging the numbers again, Dr. Childress?" I joked.

"No," John replied. "A captain has to report and chart accurate readings if it's going to be smooth sailing up ahead."

"Aye, aye, sir," I said, saluting with whichever hand was up for the task, as we chuckled at ourselves.

John filled me with three Ibuprofen before bed that night, hoping to ensure that some sleep would come my way, which it did just before midnight.

At breakfast the next morning, I asked John something that I hadn't asked him before. "Honey, how do you think it'll be when I see myself for the first time?"

John answered with caution and confidence. "Sweetie, the first time you look, it will be a shock. The second time, you'll be curious. And, the third time, you'll just say, 'Well, that's me.'"

"Honey, did you read that somewhere?" I asked. "I remember reading in that one book from Dr. Salydar to not look at myself for the first time through a mirror, but to instead, just look down at myself."

"No, I didn't read that anywhere, sweetie," John replied, thoughtfully. "But I've been thinking about when you *do* look, and that's how I imagine it will go for you, or for any woman, possibly."

God is my salvation, and John is my anchor. "You are so sweet, honey. God gave me an amazing husband," I said with joyful and thankful tears filling the pools of my eyes.

I hadn't planned it, so *God* must have planned my posing that question to John about my first look. Because quite by accident when John began draining my tube at 9:00 a.m. as I sat on the side of the bed, my eyes glanced downward and were suddenly staring, in horror, at my new body. I meant to just look down at the tube's placement, but my eyes had dove deeper and landed at the incision's breast-less site. I gasped, unable to process, recognize or believe that this was my body. John quickly stood up and wrapped his arms around me as I wept on his shoulder in complete and utter shock. It was just as John had said it would be at first sight.

"Sweetie, it's okay. It's going to heal and look a lot better than this," John said, reassuringly.

Still trying to gather myself, I took another unplanned second look—my curiosity one—and I saw that my incision went from one side of me to the other. I had been cut clear across from beneath one arm to the underside of the other.

This wasn't the depiction of the mastectomy I'd seen with John in the video at Dr. Salydar's office. And, it didn't represent any of the pictures in my brochures and pamphlets. All of those photos had shown an approximate four-inch incision only at the location of each breast. But, mine was paved clear across, without markings, indicators, or warning signs from books or by mouth that I was in for a construction site (sight) of this magnitude.

Then I remembered, still taking myself in with bewilderment, that Dr. Salydar had just returned from a conference prior to our May 6th meeting. She had told John and me about how they don't remove a bunch of lymph nodes anymore, except the ones they suspect are affected. So, it had to be that the length and radius of the mastectomy incision changed among the advancements as well. *Maybe this was a new precautionary measure. Maybe the pictures,* I thought, *are what I will look like once I do heal.* God had delivered me instant comfort in these realizations and remembrances.

"Are you alright, sweetie?" John inquired, in my lingering state of silence.

I was focusing on something else now—something I guess I hadn't noticed before because my breasts had blocked it from my view. "Honey," I remarked, "when did you and I have quintuplets?"

"What?" John replied, laughing out loud.

"Has my stomach always been this big, or do you think it's just fluid from all the medicine and anesthesia I've had?"

"Sweetie, your stomach's fine," John said, still laughing.

"Sure, it is," I said, "if you've had quintuplets! For crying out loud," I continued. "Can you believe the size of that?"

So, God drove me there—not having me pace around or continue to measure the highway of my incision—but instead, distracting me with the discovery of my air-ballooned stomach. And, *that's* the part of me that I ended up hoping was not my own. (That remains a hung jury.)

My pain persisted with the right-side tube, but John and I got through it by the unwavering grace of God. And that tube was able to be removed on Thursday, May 29th, exactly forty-eight hours after the ones that preceded it.

I only felt the insufferable removal of this last tube because it was longer than the others. When Nurse Pam said, "Breathe in," I took in air like before; but when I was done blowing out, she was still in the process of removing an extremely long tube.

I panted with fright, lifting my head from the pillow and seeing, for the first time, the long limb of the octopus that was now relentless in letting me go and giving up its *lengthy* stay.

My eyes then fell toward John whose face was paralyzed in disbelief at the never-ending tube, apparently unable to inhale and exhale properly himself.

A collective gasp filled the room as Nurse Pam, John and I all spotted the end of the tube, at last appearing, then extracted.

"Wow, I think that one must have been up around my ear canal somewhere," I said, stunned and relieved that every armed extension of the octopus was finally out of me.

"I think you're right," Nurse Pam said, giggling.

John commented to Nurse Pam, "Man, I didn't know if that thing was going to have an end to it or not."

"Yeah, I was beginning to wonder that myself," Nurse Pam concurred.

I was tubeless and happy. And, because all my tubes were out, I could take my first shower since my surgery. Tomorrow morning.

"Can I put on deodorant after my shower?" I asked Nurse Pam, excitedly.

"Just a little," she replied. "You don't want to get any deodorant in your incision. That could irritate or infect it, so be careful to just use a small amount of deodorant and none down near your incision area at all."

I reluctantly agreed, though considering the pain I'd been through with these tubes, I rethought my reluctance. I absolutely didn't want to develop an infection around my incision, so I heeded Nurse Pam's warning.

It was Friday morning, May 30th, and I was finally going to get to bathe and put on a little deodorant. But, after John and I finished breakfast, I sat on the couch procrastinating going toward the shower. Now that I could take one, I wasn't sure I wanted to. I wasn't anxious to see my new body again, and I didn't know how I was even going to wash it. Nurse Pam had told me to just lightly pat over my incision with a warm washcloth, but not to rub. I could do that, but that meant putting my hands up to my incision for the first time. And I didn't know if I could do that. But I had to. My new body wasn't *going away* anytime soon, and if I didn't take a shower and apply some deodorant soon, the people around me might.

The water pressure had to be light, as also instructed by Nurse Pam. John wanted to help me during my shower, staying close by just outside the shower door throughout the duration. And he was going to wash my back since I couldn't do any reaching, yet.

It was a great shower with good-smelling results, but as the water moved quickly down the floor's drain, I was feeling quite drained myself. I supposed it would be this way for a bit while my new body adjusted, and I adjusted to my new body.

As I looked in the bathroom mirror combing my damp hair, my eyes found their way back to my incision, now viewing it from a mirror's vantage point. "So, this is what cancer looks like," I whispered softly to myself.

But those words didn't fall on my ears alone. John had been standing outside the bathroom door, and he came in and put his hands on my shoulders as he whispered back to me, "No, this is what surviving cancer looks like."

21ST STOP *Reduce Speed Now*

TODAY WAS WEDNESDAY, June 4, 2014, and it was my first follow-up appointment with Dr. Salydar since my surgery. With the cephalopod species that had dwelled inside me now completely disposed of, I was feeling better and ready for anything . . . until John and I were sitting in front of Dr. Salydar as she read to us the Surgery Stage Report.

"The Surgery Stage Report indicates that while the cancer was in your right breast," Dr. Salydar explained, "when the lab tested your left breast, the cancer was beginning to set up there as well. It wouldn't have shown itself on any scans for about a year or so because it was in the pre-cancerous stage. So, wow, Terrie, you called the correct surgery option, girl!"

"God 'called the correct surgery option,'" I said, smiling and pointing upward.

"Well, He sure got it right," replied Dr. Salydar.

She resumed the reading of the report. The sentinel lymph node that Dr. Salydar removed and requested a second opinion on came back showing that "a fleck of a cancer cell" had been found when the lab dissected the lymph node further. The size of the fleck was described to us as being "the size of the tip of a ballpoint pen."

"With these findings," Dr. Salydar continued, "your cancer was placed under Stage Two, which is the stage that

I anticipated. But, the main reveal here that alarms me is that the cancer was moving to your left breast. And, because of that, I'm going to send your tumor off for testing to see what the chance and risk is of recurrence anywhere else in your body. I'm going to be sending that out tomorrow morning."

"Oh, so we'll know whether I need radiation or not, then," I said.

"No . . . chemo!" Dr. Salydar remarked, emphatically. Her words were unguarded, as was my heart, for this news.

I wasn't ready or prepared for this. Dr. Salydar and I hadn't really spoken of the probability of chemo, as we'd only explored the possibility of radiation. Even with the forthcoming knowledge that I knew I would gain from the Surgery Stage Report in further explaining and outlining my cancer, the scenario of needing chemo never entered my mind. But I don't know why it wouldn't have. Cancer, chemo, and radiation have always been close friends.

"Chemo?" I asked, my shocked tears breaking apart the word into more than two syllables.

"The chemotherapy would be done as a preventive measure to ward off the possibility of recurrence," stated Dr. Salydar. "If the test results from your tumor come back at high risk, you'll need to have chemo. But, if they come back at low risk, you won't need to have it. And, we should get the results back in about two weeks."

John's soft voice embraced me as he asked Dr. Salydar, "What about the 'fleck of a cancer cell' that was found? Will that factor in and determine her need for chemo as well?"

The shell of me sat there as the word, chemo, bounced off and around me like a ball inside of an arcade game. The ball was chemo, and I was its primary target, depending on my score of 'high risk' or 'low risk' or no risk at all if the fleck was to be part of the consideration.

"She wouldn't need chemo for the fleck. And, while I don't expect that there's a fleck anywhere else because it was so small," Dr. Salydar commented, "the oncologist and Dr. Dewitt in radiation will decide if they think that radiation is warranted on the right side where I removed the lymph node."

"Oncologist?" I asked, my tears bursting in surprise again.

"Yes," Dr. Salydar said. "They're all so good that I can't even handpick the best one for you. I will have Nurse Pam set you up an appointment with one so you can go ahead and meet. You will take hormone therapy—Tamoxifen— and your oncologist will get you started on that after the test results come in. We need to wait for those first."

I pushed my tears aside so that I could speak as I prepared to ask a fuller question. "Will I only stay with the oncologist if I need to have chemo, and to get started on the Tamoxifen?"

"Oh, no," replied Dr. Salydar. "You'll have an oncologist that you'll see every four to five months for the next five years, regardless of the results. Because you'll be taking hormone therapy for five years, you'll need to be monitored and checked throughout that duration. You'll have blood work drawn each time you see the oncologist that will convey your white blood cell count, make sure the Tamoxifen is doing its job, and to keep check on your Vitamin D levels."

Dr. Salydar asked if John or I had any more questions. John said no. I could no longer speak to reply, so I nodded no.

As Dr. Salydar prepared to leave, she hugged me and said she'd see me again in December. I was certain that I had heard her wrong, so I repeated that month back to her. She confirmed that I had heard her correctly. "But you will call me in two weeks with the results?" I asked, frightened to know and not wanting to know all at once.

"You'll hear from me in two weeks," Dr. Salydar assured. "I'm sending it off tomorrow morning, so it should be two weeks from tomorrow that we'll know."

On my way out, the girl at the desk gave me the phone number to contact physical therapy, as Dr. Salydar wanted me to go ahead and begin my sessions for wound care, reach regain, and lymphedema prevention. Nurse Pam turned the corner and told me that she would contact the oncology department and call me with my oncologist's name and appointment date.

Dr. Salydar also decided that I could go ahead and be fitted for prosthetics whenever I felt up to it. My surgery had only been two weeks ago. But I wasn't seeming to keep up with as fast as other things were unfolding around me. The one thing that was obvious to me, though—I wasn't up for a prosthetic fitting today. I would have to wait and do that another time.

John was reassuring and very consoling on our walk out to the car. "Sweetie, either way, you're going to be fine. God has gotten you through the hardest part—the surgery—and you did great through that," he reminded.

I looked over at John as my seatbelt clicked over top of my flower pillow. "But what if that wasn't the hardest part? What if," I hesitated, "the treatments are the hardest part? What if losing my hair, after losing my breasts, is the hardest part?"

John took my hand as my tears continued a waterfall down the front of my flat shirt. And in his soft calm voice of reason, he said, "Sweetie, you'll still be living in spite of those things. You'll still be up walking around, living your life. You'll be living your life with me. It's you and me, all the way, my Navy SEAL."

He kissed my hand as my cascading stream splashed over onto him.

"Honey, I'm thinking that you're the Navy SEAL," I

finally confessed, "and I'm just in training with you as my compassionate Senior Chief petty officer."

As we pulled away from the parking lot, fear quickly overtook me as my thoughts of the uncertainty ahead tugged at me and took me back to that dark place that I had visited earlier when I was in the hotel room.

God was there with His broom last time, and He was knocking on the door to be let in this time. But I thought I needed to give my mind the chance to explore the dark possibilities. And the more I thought, the more paralyzed by my fear I became.

We approached a traffic light, and as we slowed to a stop, I began observing people around us—those pouring from sidewalks in either direction crossing beneath the swinging light, and those sitting in their cars nearby.

I watched these people from inside my shadowy bubble where they couldn't see into me. I stared at the world of others living, laughing, and enjoying life, but I didn't feel like I was a part of them anymore. Even though I could clearly see them, I felt like I was somewhere else, something else, headed elsewhere by myself to a dismal corner that only I had been summoned to occupy.

My watchful eyes stayed on the busyness and business of others as I thought, *My life hangs in the balance, but theirs* . . . God's knock grew louder at the door. *Theirs,* I thought, *also does. This can happen to any of us even though we think it never will. That's why we have to make every day count! God lives in our joy, and in our sorrow; so, our walk regardless of the road we're on, is never longer than what we can tread. God treks with us to make sure we complete every journey that's laid out before us.*

I suddenly began to wonder what cross each of these people among me was carrying and how different of paths we were really on. They didn't know about me any more than I knew about them.

My apprehension took a break from me for a moment as it allowed me to contemplate the reality of the unknown for others. None of us know what tomorrow will bring.

As John made the turn under the green light, my up-close eyeshot of others fell to the rearview mirror. My gazing was over, and the hands of trepidation lunged at me once again, demanding my attention and beckoning me back to my own unknown.

I let my mind finally open the door that my thoughts had locked me from, permitting God and His broom to reenter. Peace rushed in as I heard God whisper, "You're going to get through this. Trust Me."

22ND STOP *Slow Down*

I N THE NEXT week, I went and got my hair cut, and I loved it. But I tried not to get used to it, still awaiting the news of my test results. For I was resolving myself to the fact that every strand of hair on my head, all with a slight wave, may each have to wave goodbye to me in a matter of days. But, my and John's 17th wedding anniversary and my 50th birthday was coming up, and I would have my hair for those occasions. So, all was well, for now.

Despite the dubious cloud that hung above both our heads, John and I had a wonderful anniversary at Montpelier, the historic home of James and Dolley Madison. My eyes and thoughts were set only on my sweetheart husband and my gratefulness to God for another year celebrating our marriage.

I turned fifty just two days later. And, I got the best birthday present in the world from God at 12:14 a.m., just minutes after entering this new decade of my life.

John and I were lying in bed talking about some different places to go, as he wanted to take me somewhere special for my 50th birthday. John's words, all at once, became muffled and distant as God's tranquil voice cut in, "Your test results are going to come back low risk."

I couldn't believe what I just clearly heard, as if John, himself, had announced it. I lifted my head and looked at John as he continued to roll off names of places we could visit. I excitedly interrupted him, "My test results are going to come back low risk!"

"What?" John said, as he looked at me with his head now lifted from his pillow.

"God just told me. It was clear as a bell. *Happy 50th birthday to me*," I sang, lying my head back down. "Best! Gift! Ever!" I declared, with utter joy.

"Sweetie, are you sure?" John asked, looking at me as if I had lost the icing off my cake, so to speak.

"I'm sure. My results are going to come back low risk. I got it straight from the Great Physician, Himself," I confirmed, most assuredly.

"Well now, isn't that something. I guess we'll wait and see. But I know that God's been speaking to you and giving you small nudges so that you'd know what to do on each thing you've had to decide. So, we'll celebrate big today in anticipation of low risk results *and* your 50th birthday!" John proclaimed.

John took me to the home and garden tour of James Monroe at Ashlawn-Highland for my birthday. It was a perfect day and one of the best birthdays I'd ever had. My 48th and 49th before it, however, were a very different story.

Both of those previous birthdays had found me sad at morning's rise, and even weepy-eyed throughout most of the day. For some reason, and quite abruptly, I had begun not liking my birthday. I pondered whether it was because I was getting closer to the age of fifty. Though I still don't know if that was exactly it or not. But I remember making a profound statement as John and I walked through a parking lot in Middleburg on my 49th birthday. "I hate my birthday. I wish I didn't have to have anymore."

Yeah, God heard that. And I knew that He had used my cancer as another lesson in this arena to remind me what having no more birthdays would really mean and feel like. He had already revealed to me again and again in my journey the blessings of life that a birthday can bring. And, I was never going to disregard that bounty ever again. Another year of life *is* the gift we get *from God*, every year a new birthday comes around.

23ʀᴅ STOP *Changing Lanes*

TODAY, JUNE 25, 2014, was the day I would find out if I needed to have chemo or not. Dr. Salydar was going to pass along the results to my oncologist, Dr. Ritter, since I was scheduled to see him today. I prepared myself for whichever side of the page the news fell upon. Or at least, I thought I did. When Dr. Ritter entered the examination room where John and I were awaiting the results, he delivered us word on something that wasn't even an option.

"Um..." Dr. Ritter began, glancing back and forth from me to the floor as he spoke. "I don't have any results for you. Nothing was sent out."

"What?" I replied, in disbelief. "I know my tumor was sent out, and I can tell you the date it was sent—Thursday, June 5ᵗʰ, before noon."

"You know that, for sure?" Dr. Ritter asked, now surprised himself.

"Yes," I said, confidently. "Dr. Salydar made mention twice the day of my follow-up appointment with her on June 4ᵗʰ that she was absolutely going to be sending the tumor off the next morning. That's how I know that it went out on June 5ᵗʰ. So, it had to be sent."

"Since you know the date, then," Dr. Ritter said, "let me go call Dr. Salydar again. I'll be right back."

As Dr. Ritter left the room, I looked over at John, who

for the first time on this journey was red-faced and angry. "How could it not have been sent?" John pondered, loudly out loud.

"I can't imagine that Dr. Salydar didn't send it. There's got to be an explanation," I pondered back.

My soft John boomed, "Well, if it wasn't sent out, there better be a really good explanation."

Here's the thing about the sudden change in my calm-natured husband. When John's doing business, of any kind, he expects efficient and professional service. We both grew up in the time of those principle ethics and were, in fact, groomed to provide those very foundations whenever we were rendering services in our own professions. And in addition to that, this was John's pilgrimage, too.

We sat quietly after that, waiting and wading around in our own separate thoughts and discernments; so, when Dr. Ritter reappeared, neither John nor I even flinched, consumed by our individual pensiveness.

"It wasn't sent," Dr. Ritter commented, softly, as he closed the door behind him. "I don't know if it was forgotten or what, but I'm going to be in charge of sending it out now. And I'm going to work to get you the results quickly, so you don't have to wait another two to three weeks. I'm really sorry this happened."

"*How* did this happen?" I asked, becoming more unglued myself.

"And, *why* did this happen?" John echoed, still unraveling as well.

"I don't know, and I'm sorry that I don't know," Dr. Ritter replied, embarrassed and sympathetic at the same time.

John's concern dove deeper from a medical perspective than mine, as he posed a great question. "Will the tumor still have been preserved enough for the lab to get a good sample, or does it have to be tested within a certain timeframe before it starts to expire and give off false or inaccurate readings?"

"The tumor has been frozen and remains as such, so it will most certainly still be preserved and will provide definitive results," remarked Dr. Ritter.

"How will I know it's my tumor that has been sent off and not someone else's at this point?" I asked, not imagining that I would ever have to ask that question.

"Your name is tagged to the bag that contains your tumor, so there will be no mistake that it will be *yours*," Dr. Ritter said, with certainty.

The room was silent for only a moment when John asked, "Who do I need to go punch in the nose for this?"

I could tell by the look on John's face that he was serious and actually wanted to be supplied with a name.

"I wish I knew," Dr. Ritter said, also appearing to want to converse with a punching bag. "The ball could have been dropped by anyone—the doctor, the nurse, a staff member, someone in the lab—it's hard to say."

"Well, I want you to investigate what happened, and I want to know who's responsible for 'dropping this ball,'" my Rambo husband replied.

"I will do that, and I will let you know," Dr. Ritter commented, "because I want to know that myself."

A calm reassurance and realization fell over me as we left Dr. Ritter's office, and I shared these epiphanies with John in hopes of settling him as well.

I knew that these feelings and thoughts were mixtures in the wet blacktop of a *Private Drive* that God had just freshly laid for my following reflections: My cancer had been found at an early stage; the cancer removed was only two centimeters in diameter; and, my surgery had taken place. So, my circumstances weren't dire. If this mistake had to happen to somebody, I was resolved in the gladness that it had happened to me instead of someone who needed to know their results *yesterday*. I could wait a little longer, but had this fallacy happened to someone else with a more severe scenario, they may not, literally, have been able to wait. And besides, I really had already gotten word of my results from God in the early morning hours of my birthday just two days ago. So, it was time to hang on to *that* word . . . God's word.

Dr. Ritter had promised us that the tumor would be "sent out first thing" the next morning. And it was, because a week and a half later, the phone call came from him ringing these words from the phone receiver, "Your test results came back low risk." (I wanted to say that I already knew that.) "So, no chemo for you! Actually, the results came back very low risk, showing that you're in the eighth percentile of any recurrence," Dr. Ritter continued.

I had to break that last part down into Layman's terms as I repeated back to Dr. Ritter, "So, 'the eighth percentile' means that I have only an 8% chance of recurrence?"

"That's correct," replied Dr. Ritter.

When I hung up, John and I embraced, tears leaking from both of us. "See?" I whispered in John's ear, "I told you that God said my test results were going to come back low risk."

John looked at me. "That's right. So, you really did hear Him that night."

"Yes, I did," I faithfully said.

While John and I were elated with the results, when we met with Dr. Ritter a week after his phone call, John asked what he had learned about the delay in the tumor not being sent out on its original date of June 5th. Dr. Ritter informed us that it was still under review and that he had advised the hospital administration of the blunder.

"But we know the results now, honey," I said quickly in an

attempt to water down the eminent fire that I saw beginning to flame up again in John.

"That's true," John replied. "But this doesn't need to happen again to someone else."

"Well, in my conversation with the administration," Dr. Ritter continued, "they told me that they would take the appropriate measures to ensure that something like this doesn't happen again."

"Well, it shouldn't happen again," my warm John smoldered.

I think that God eventually doused John with some water or sprayed him with a cool mist from His Heaven, because we all left the room shaking hands, laughing, and exchanging grateful words upon our departure.

Dr. Ritter had told me that he and the radiation oncologist had met and decided that I wouldn't need any radiation for the fleck that had been found in the lymph node that was removed. He and Dr. Dewitt had concurred that the chance of there being another fleck inside me was "nil to zero."

In light of that decision and the need for no chemo, I could begin taking the hormone therapy, Tamoxifen. Dr. Ritter warned of the main side effect being hot flashes, "but other than that," he had said, "you shouldn't have any problems with it."

Tamoxifen was to help lessen the threat of cancer returning, so taking one each day was important. And among the other pills I already took, this one would be the one that I was most thankful for.

So, these were my current treatment road lanes: Tamoxifen and physical therapy.

Though as a few more months passed, Dr. Ritter discovered from a series of blood panels that my cancer was estrogen-driven. This revelation prompted my needing to have chemo shots—once a month for five to six months—in an effort to shut down my ovaries.

While the chemo shots caused slight hair loss and balding just at the top right crown of my head, they were unsuccessful in idling the ovaries. *Rats! And, hair balls!* I thought to myself. More maintenance would be required in the mechanics of things.

So, my next surgery ensued in the form of a total hysterectomy as put in motion by my exceptional and 'best-in-the-business' team of physicians, with God unyielding in the driver's seat.

The roads ahead unforeseen by us are so much smoother when we just let go of the steering wheel and let God drive . . . while we play passenger.

24TH STOP Bump (The Roadside Brawl)

I T WAS SEPTEMBER 6, 2014, and it arose as a good day. I went to work in my church library, ran some errands, ate lunch out with John, caught up on my Bible meditations, and started reading a new book entitled, *The Giver*.

As I sat there reading, I thought, *what a perfect synonymous name for God—The Giver, because of all He has given us and continues to give us every day.* And, the story line was even an ideal match.

In Lois Lowry's tale, The Giver is the person who can provide memories, joy, pain and suffering, nature in color with all its beautiful surroundings, family, friends, hope, healing, emotions and abilities. God gave us those in real life, while the character of The Giver reminds us of the depth and acknowledgement of receiving them again. God is real; The Giver is fiction. But, the truth of the matter is fact in both. We know and have these things because of The One who gave them to us: God, The Giver of life.

I didn't feel moody today like I'd been in the past couple weeks; though, maybe a little. In retrospect, the biblical connection of my reading in *The Giver* had seemed to quiet and soothe my soul. And, the gripping storm inside me earlier had definitely settled from previous days.

I was never a moody person before the tumultuous

thundering of Tamoxifen was added to the soft rain shower of my demeanor. Luckily, its hard pounding hadn't lasted beyond two weeks. But, before its wounding effect had begun to leave me, it allowed me to get in a few good punches with an unlikely opponent late one evening.

For the first time since my original prosthetic fitting and purchase back in June, I decided to retry on my bra and prosthetic forms that had idly sat boxed behind the armoire doors awaiting their rematch with me.

I gently lifted the forms from their fancy silk-lined boxes, paying particular attention to which one was marked, Left, and which one was Right. If I forgot, they were lightly stamped with an L and R on the underside.

The imagery of Edna, the fitter, sliding the forms inside the bra pockets began to play in single snapshots in my head as I mimicked her movements. *First the left, then the right. Make sure they're centered. There. That's it.* They felt like bowling balls as I lifted the heavyweight bra up from the bed and against my flattened center.

Hooking the bra felt foreign to me, as I hadn't hooked a bra for three and a half months. But, after my first failed attempt to link together the hooks, my second try was 'like getting back up on the seat of a bike after you've fallen off.' Or something like that, just without the original seat!

All looked well until I slipped on my shirt to view the new landscape. I was hoping for a knockout. But it was more like a takeout. My left breast form was slightly, but obviously, bigger than my right one from both the side and front profiles. When I went to model for John, he quickly noticed the size difference, too.

I went back into the bedroom and took off the bra so I could reposition the left form. When I replaced the canvas of my shirt back upon it, there was no difference. And worse,

I could feel the left strap pricking at my tight skin like a hornet's nest of angry bees. I quickly peeled the shirt and stinging heavyweight bra from my body. I laid the bra, still filled with the forms, on the bed and squatted down, staring at the lopsided left prosthetic, eye to fake boob. *This form is no match for me,* I thought. *Literally, it's no match. How could I wear this?* Its off sizes even made the bra look wrong and feel uncomfortable.

I was going to make it work and make it right. I had to. I'd had them, I thought, too long to exchange and request a re-fitting. (I didn't know it then, but I was wrong about that.) The only option in my mind, at the time, was to have a bout with this left form. I could feel the anger traveling down my hands, providing each finger a strength they'd never possessed before in order to make the hits count. So, the swinging of punches, mashes, and flattening blows began and were thrown one after another from my empowered fists to the boastful left-breasted form.

And, after the first round, I watched as the left form rose to the occasion of the next anticipated strike. It continued to blossom back to its original shape each time after three rounds of hard pummeling. I threw in the towel. I gave up in defeat and gathered the champion opponent into my arms and tossed it (my final attempt to win the match) back into the armoire. Keeping the armoire doors open, I sat on the bed and stared at it. I guess I thought my piercing glare might somehow deflate it. However, the left form stood proud, taking me out in three rounds without even as much as a scratch on it.

I was the only one bruised in the *brawl*—my esteem, my vanity, my pride, and my new flat uncovered boxing ring, (a.k.a. my chest). I wanted to cry, but it was as if someone had turned off the *plumbing* inside of me. In my self-pity,

I thought, *Great. Another 'needs repair' sign hanging over my head.*

My need to cry and inability to do so led me to further frustration inside myself. This storm was impactful, but I knew that God was the steady stillness that would take and calm me in the hindsight of its passing. And, He's always known that I never really looked good in boxing gloves, anyway.

25TH STOP *Expect Delays on Tuesday, 11/14/14*

JOHN AND I arrived a bit early Friday afternoon, November 14, 2014, for my next appointment with Dr. Ritter. As we entered toward the check-in window, we heard the voice of a very happy, and quite entertaining, gentleman also checking in nearby. I caught the eye of a nurse I knew sitting at the next window over, signaling me to check in with her.

Once I was signed in, John and I took a seat among a small smattering of other waiting patients. As we sat on the couch facing the Infusion Center, also known as the chemotherapy center, my thoughts drifted to imagining how things would have gone if I had needed intravenous chemo. God had allowed me to pass that intersection when my test results of reoccurrence came back 'low risk.' But as I sat there envisioning myself on the other side of that glass, I wondered, *how would I have felt walking through that door the first time? Would I have gotten sick from the chemo? Would my treatments be over now? What would I look like? Thin? Bald? Pale? Cured?*

Then, my thoughts immediately shifted to those who *were* undergoing chemotherapy and how they must feel, think, and live their lives in this new ordinary. I wanted so much to do something for them, all of them, especially those who were going it alone without family or a friend by their side. *When my energy returns more and my incision is better healed,*

I'm going to do something for them, I silently promised myself and those sitting behind the drawn curtains.

As my thoughts continued to stir with ideas of how I could serve others, my placid bubble and the quietness of the waiting area was burst with the resonating clap of that happy man, still standing at the check-in station. He was shouting to all who would look and listen, "I'm wearing the map of the world!"

As most of us turned our curious heads toward him, he stood beaming back at us, arms outstretched, holding open his coat to expose the inside lining that did, indeed, have a landscaped 'map of the world' printed across its fabric. Some laughed, some smiled, and others just returned their eyes back toward the floor, considering what they had just seen. Although John was engrossed in a magazine, he was well aware of the presence of this man, who soon came to join our side of the waiting room.

Everything had once again fallen back into silence as we all sat waiting our turn to be called. Another husband and wife had arrived and sat down across from us. And, in a near corner facing us, was the broken smile of missing teeth grinning back at us that belonged to the man who was wrapped in the map of the world. His eye catching mine caused him to break the hushed room again. When he spoke, he spoke loudly, but I don't believe it was to attract an audience at all. His volume just seemed of one trying to be heard, not necessarily of one wanting to be.

"I have this burning question in my head," he said. "What is a pancreas and what does it do?"

With no other voices responding, I replied, "The pancreas is an organ that helps to digest food." As the words left my mouth, I questioned every one of them, not so much for my replying but for the accuracy of my response.

"Well," he went on, "I had an MRI of my pancreas yesterday and was told it was swollen. I was glad to hear I wasn't pregnant, because I didn't know where things might come out on that."

That remark got John's attention. He looked up from his magazine, laughed, nodded back to the man, and said, "Well, that's really good news!"

The man laughed and commented back, "I'm here every Tuesday. No, not really," he jested. "I'm sorry. I don't mean to be talking so much. I just can't be quiet. My mom always told me I talked too much. I'm just having a really good day, and I'm here every Tuesday."

As he continued to speak during our waiting period, his voice would soften to quieter notes now and then.

"So, have you ever heard of the Wounded Warrior Project?" he asked, looking at John and me.

We responded in unison, "Yes."

"Well, I'm on a fixed income, but I give $19.00 a month to that project. Did you know that the other day was Veteran's Day?"

"We did," I replied. "Are you a veteran?"

"Oh, yes, ma'am. I was in the Navy and the Army. I . . ."

Tuesday, as I now thought of him, was interrupted by the nurse's next calling out of a patient's name.

Serenity fell once more in the waiting arena. I sat curious of what Tuesday's story was or would be. And, would he be going it alone? I was determined to find out at some point.

The next sound was the nurse's calling of my name. As John and I stood to follow her, I looked at Tuesday and said, "You keep having a good day."

"I will," he said, smiling back with that priceless, almost toothless, grin.

I left the waiting room not knowing his real name, but he

looked like a Tuesday. A day of the week not so popular, but just as important as any other day of the week. Tuesday had a place in the order of things. And another new day couldn't proceed without Tuesday.

26TH STOP End Road Work

A s I LOOK back on my journey through cancer, I feel like my life has been consecrated and renewed in so many ways. While no one would ever choose or want to travel cancer's highway, including me, God has taxied me to amazing experiences and incredible people that I wouldn't have had the honor of crossing, otherwise. And, I wouldn't trade those opportunities for the world.

I have also cruised a new inroad of spiritual growth and overwhelming appreciation in my faith and relationship with God and others because of all the road signs that God led me to and thru along the tight turns. When I stop and think about it, most road signs are like messages from God as He shapes and escorts us through a life that is continually *Under Construction.*

God has enriched my life with more meaning and purpose than I ever could have imagined, and I can feel Him using me for His will, not mine, and guiding my every direction and decision.

'Taking time to stop and smell the flowers' is an understatement of how much I embrace everything around me now. I've worn glasses for years but am seeing through them differently and noticing things, small things, that my lenses didn't seem to have in focus before. And, I wonder if they're God's spectacles I'm looking through at times?

(Although, I'm pretty sure that He has 20/20 vision and wouldn't need eyewear.)

I used to be one of those people who thought that cancer would never happen to me. Despite my family tree blowing leaves of vivid possibility into my path, I felt immune, safe, and even a giant in comparison to the idea of cancer. So, there I was living my life, walking through my daily routines, and playing a giant. But then, cancer wanted to be the giant, replacing my world with its monstrous own while mocking a woman who had once played a giant. Though as time goes by, I'm comfortably wearing the mask that tried to wear me— both minute versions now. Because as it turns out, me as the first giant, and the second giant (cancer) that was after me, wasn't as huge as God.

"Our trials are great opportunities, but all too often we simply see them as large obstacles (giants). If only we would recognize every difficult situation as something God has chosen to prove His love to us, each obstacle would then become a place of shelter and rest and a demonstration to others of His inexpressible power. If we would look for the signs of His glorious handiwork, then every cloud would indeed become a rainbow, and every difficult mountain path would become one of ascension, transformation and glorification. If we would look at our past, most of us would realize that the times we endured the greatest stress and felt that every path was blocked were the very times our heavenly Father chose to do the kindest things for us and bestow His richest blessings."—A.B. Simpson, NIV Streams in the Desert.

Had I not toured this path with God, I would never have experienced the capacity of His blessings and known the depth of His love and infinite power in the giant dwarfness of cancer.

As far as life in the new vehicle that is my body, I'm driving well and maintaining regular check-ups. So, I'm 'running like a top.' In fact, so well, that I sometimes forget that the front wheels that balanced me are missing, especially as I go about my morning dressing routine only to find myself wobbling around inside the closet like one of those round-bottomed inflatable clowns. I never thought about my breasts being my in-balance, though I was advised by my physical therapist, Marcy, that it may take some time for me to feel fully aligned without them.

One evening at the dinner table, the absence of my breasts was completely neglected by my memory as I reached across my plate to pick up a jar of applesauce that was sitting near John. I gasped, "Oh no! I think I just dipped my breast into my plate. Oh, wait a minute . . . I don't have that one anymore. Never mind, I'm good."

John just shook his head and smiled at me. I think that I joke, in part, to 'accept the things I cannot change' as well as an acquired skill I learned from my father. Daddy would use humor in a serious situation just to lighten things up and make the circumstance seem not so serious. And, while it didn't change the importance of things, it could make it less worrisome and more bearable. If even for a moment.

Marcy and I met twice a week for seven months for lunges and laughter, stretches and 'photo shoots,' and massages and mayhem. My time and chapter with her ended with making small adjustments in exchange for abundant blessings.

One small adjustment is that while my reach is back, it is at a slight forward slant, because the skin beneath my arms remains numb and tight, leaving my reach for things up high or far across a bit of a challenge. Though, that could rebound in time, giving me my full reach back. And, with the at-home exercises that Marcy provided for me, I believe that's *reachable*!

Even though my road work is done for now, the truth is that we are all a 'work in progress.' God is always patterning us to make sure that in our travels as we encounter people along the way who need Him, that we are ready to turn our lights on *for* Him and help guide others through the dark tunnels *toward* Him.

Though, I still find myself wondering if cancer will impart its shadow across my clear windshield again someday, nevertheless, this expedition of love and lessons alongside God was worth the ride. And we all have God's promise on every thoroughfare with Him, *"For I know the thoughts that I think toward you, says the Lord, thoughts of peace and not of evil, to give you a future and a hope. Then you will call upon Me and go and pray to Me, and I will listen to you. You will seek Me and find Me when you search for Me with all your heart."*—Jeremiah 29:11-13, NKJV Holy Bible.

AFTERWORD
Drive Safely

THINGS HAPPEN EVERY day that we can't explain that stop us in our tracks, stifle our souls, silence our words, split our hearts, and haze the normal flow of life as we know it. We search for something to hold on to—something to anchor us and keep us grounded—that will encourage us to take the next step, put movement back into our soul, help us find our voice and defog our new normal.

Standing in the midst of all of the unexplainable is God . . . our tour guide, our defroster, the composer of our soul, our tongue, and our seamstress. He is our chauffeur through all of life's ups and downs, and around all the winding roads in between. And, faith is the strap that keeps us fastened and secure in Him.

By our faith, we are never alone or apart from God, not even for a second. I had always heard that but never truly grasped the real meaning or reality of it until my cancer diagnosis. They were words that I gave little thought to; and then, they became words that I lived by.

Any one of us has the capability of hearing God's whispers and feeling His nudges to guide our ways, and all we have to do is ask. Then, listen. I had never experienced God in this way before my life was turned *This Way*. And now, I listen for

Him and await His reply or feel Him pushing my thoughts toward His will and want for me.

I prayed to Him just minutes before I began writing this chapter, asking Him to prepare me for my writing time and inviting Him to join me at my desk. He immediately responded by scrolling the entire two beginning paragraphs of this chapter through my mind. (I really need to think about putting a pen and notepad in the bathroom when I pray in there.)

Faith and trust go hand in hand with God. For, we can never envision what the far side of a difficult situation will look like. I couldn't picture what I would be like or look like on the other side of my mastectomy, because I'd never journeyed it. But God knew. He had scouted this path ahead of me and seen me on it so that He could lead me through it by no control or compass of my own other than to *trust* Him and remain *faithful* in that trust.

So, the secret is that there is no secret. You just have to give everything to God, then let it go and allow Him to deal with it fully and completely. Having faith in God means that *"you don't have to see the whole staircase, just take the first step."*—Dr. Martin Luther King, Jr.

When we are met with a roadblock, God uses that detour to give us a more purposeful life—a life where we understand and embrace joy even more because we've known real sorrow. Without the clouds, we would never know the power of the Son. And our blessings are the sequels to our trials.

The God who made us knows what we need when we need it. Our faith in Him is a daily reminder that He is, indeed, in charge of our lives and circumstances, if we only entrust ourselves to Him.

"Many years ago, there was a monk who needed olive oil, so he planted an olive tree sapling. Once it was planted, he

prayed, 'Lord, my tree needs rain so its tender roots may drink and grow.' And, the Lord sent gentle showers. Then, the monk prayed for the Lord to send sun, and the sun shone gilding the once-dripping clouds. 'Now, send frost, dear Lord, to strengthen its branches.' And soon the little tree was covered in sparkling frost, but by evening it had died. Then the monk sought out a brother monk and told him of his strange experience. After hearing the story, the other monk said, 'I also planted a little tree. See how it's thriving! But I entrust my tree to its God. He who made it knows better than a man like me what it needs. I gave God no constraints or conditions, except to ask Him to send what it needs—whether that be a storm or sunshine, wind, rain, or frost. You made it, and You know best what it needs.'"—L.B. Cowman, NIV Streams in the Desert.

"Truly I tell you, if you have faith as small as a mustard seed, you can say to this mountain, 'Move from here to there,' and it will move. Nothing will be impossible for you."—Matthew 17:20, NIV Streams in the Desert.

Challenge your mountain in the Lord! He has climbed them all, and none of them are too tall, too steep, or too impossible for Him to carry you across.

"Therefore, may we continue to persevere, for even if we took our circumstances and cast all the darkness of human doubt upon them and then hastily piled as many difficulties together as we could find against God's divine work, we could never move beyond the blessedness of His miracle-working power.

May we place our faith completely in Him, for He is the God of the impossible."—L.B. Cowman, NIV Streams in the Desert.

SUPPLEMENT
Driver's Ed. (Advanced Lesson): Fishing Tales and Humbling Fly Ties

THERAPEUTIC ADVENTURES' *Spring Fly Fling Women's Fly-Fishing Retreat* weekend event of April 2015, led and organized by its God-appointed founder, Mark Andrews, for cancer survivors was an enchanting weekend that I'll never forget. Not only because of the rustic accommodations, therapeutic amenities, gourmet meals, amazing guides and volunteers, live musical entertainment, (did I mention gourmet food?), and majestic mountain views framing a wide picturesque lake, but because of the unity formed among seven women and their stories that wove us in a common thread as if we'd known each other all our lives. It was like a reunion without the first introduction. And, we became bound together quickly as we paralleled in strength and fortitude, though our cancer walks were all very different.

The motto for this event was "Match the Hatch with Fighting Spirit." I originally thought that meant for us to 'match the hatch' with as many catches as there were fish (that had been placed in the river for us) using our newly learned fly-fishing skills. But I found out later that its real meaning was the abundance of fish that had been added to the river was appropriated to match our overflowing determination, faith, and perseverance. We were the ones that the countless fish were trying to match. Wow! I never thought I would feel so honored to be looked up to by a fish, and by the hands of those who had placed them there. For me, God was the true recipient of this honor, and I was His proud vessel.

And, something else that 'matched the hatch' among us seven women were our blessings from God. While our cancer excursions led each of us down a diverse and differing path, the blessings at the end of our tunnels were completely equal in their rich healing and memorable rides.

As my new friends and I gathered around a picnic table of wine and hors d'oeuvres on a patio deck overlooking the lake, the storytelling of our journeys began. The stories became cast together in a river of variations as the lines commenced, becoming entwined as if they'd been waiting to meet at the same fishing hole for some time.

Our conversations continued to cross the table encircling our dinner plates as several women shared their stories of chemo—the life it restored in them, and the hair, eyelashes, and eyebrows it took from them, and kept from them, for a while. Some of the women had lustrous short hair. (I would love for my hair to lay, for just one day, as beautifully as theirs did, as my hair always looks like I have a hilltop peaking on each side as my cowlicks bud like dogwoods.)

When Lauren glanced across the table at me and asked how my chemo went, my heart sank as I replied, "Well, I didn't have to have chemo. My test results for recurrence came back low risk in the eighth percentile of chance. And, while I was glad that I didn't have to have chemo, my heart was heavy for those who did. So, the sword of 'no chemo' news was kind of double-edged for me in my reflections of others whose results were opposite. My cancer was caught fairly early, and I had a bilateral mastectomy without reconstruction."

As all of the women seated around the table had now turned their attention on me, I used the next moment to lighten things up, and, provide a 'heads up' to them by announcing, "Now, if any of you happen to see me from the side profile this weekend and you notice a totally flat top area here," as I gestured at my chest, "with a large mountain beneath it (my stomach), it's not an optical illusion, and your eyes aren't playing tricks on you. It's just me not wearing my prosthetic breasts, because Edna said, 'Terrie, whatever you do, DON'T get these wet!' So, I didn't pack them."

Ripples of laughter broke out into the crisp mountain air, and even my own chuckling escaped into the coolness, maybe because of the brutal honesty of being comfortable in my own skin, and the light-heartedness that we all had in the acceptance of our newly chiseled bodies that now fulfilled us.

Lauren and I sprang back into our original conversation about chemo, as she stated, "You are so sweet. But you shouldn't feel bad that you didn't have chemo with the rest of us. I'm glad you didn't need to have it. So, did you have radiation?"

"That conversation," I commented, "was discussed among two oncologists at least twice, that I'm aware of, regarding my need for radiation. What they called a 'fleck' was detected in the sentinel node that was taken during my surgery. And after much deliberation and thought, they agreed that it would not be feasible or necessary for me to have radiation therapy. My oncologist even remarked to me that the chance of there being another fleck inside me somewhere else was 'nil to zero.'" That was it. That was my short story.

I suddenly felt a pang of guilt having not had either treatment injected into me as these amazing women had

had. And, it wasn't because I was being made to feel this way by them at all. It was internally and personally me. I just wanted to be on the same plateau of understanding and knowledge with these ladies who had greatly and harshly endured the side effects of these manipulative therapies. But as we continued to reveal our accounts, I quickly realized that the thoughts, feelings, and fears that traveled through each of us during our bouts with cancer carried the exact same identity.

As the tales of my new friends more fully unfolded, each narrative was in contrast of the other, and some much more difficult.

Carol's story:

Out of the group, Carol's cancer was the most similar to mine, and like me, she didn't need to have chemo. But she did have radiation. The rest of her story was silent to my ears, as I never heard her say what kind of surgery she had. Though she was a picture of health and a happy, but quiet, soul, which made me believe that her chronicle had a happy and satisfying ending.

Carol's *quietness* divulged itself as *concern* later when she shared with us that her sister had just recently been diagnosed with breast cancer. Carol's worry about her sister fell more toward the care and treatment side of things, as she communicated that her sister didn't really believe in worldly medicinal practices.

"I would just do what Dr. Salydar told me to do, what she recommended," Carol explained. "My sister is exploring medical options, but I don't think that's the planned path she'll likely take. Even the thought of having surgery would be 'out' for her."

I think we all deadpanned at this news with compassioned faces that uttered reassuring words of hope to Carol with our whole-hearted belief that her sister would find trust, contentment, and solace inside one of the medical options along her path of exploration. Our words and thoughts to Carol were spoken and felt in one accord.

Carol and I shadowed each other a lot, riding in the same vehicles with the guides to and from the Moorman River for our fishing expedition, and then wanting the same next amenity offering, all the while soaking up every piece of nature around us. And on Sunday, she and I trekked the tall mountain's uphill landscape, as we climbed side by side, at times holding onto each other, during our guided hike.

Carol and I continued to find each other in the same spots, interested in the same things at the same times throughout the weekend. She was like a sister I didn't know I had.

Sherry's story:

Sherry was diagnosed in April of 2014 with triple negative breast cancer. Triple negative means that the hormone receptors—estrogen, progesterone, and Her2—were negative.

Sherry was one of the bright spots in the weekend because of her unyielding spirit and steadfast example of strength that had faced off with cancer and won! And, she did it with a sense of wit and humor that I don't even think she realized she possessed.

Sherry had a bilateral mastectomy with reconstruction, and just to let all of us know that she was blessed and totally proud of her new body, she sported a pink t-shirt with the words, YES, THEY ARE FAKE! MY REAL ONES TRIED TO KILL ME. *Well said, sweet Sherry. You go, girl!* I thought to myself. She and that shirt seemed to be on their own mission of depicting what hope and survival looked like!

I had the pleasure of sitting with Sherry on a sun-warmed bench perched up against the outside lodge during our Saturday luncheon. As we portioned through more pieces of our cancer history, Sherry's eyes fell to the deck floor as she began telling me about the most difficult day of her cancer walk. It was not what I expected.

"The hardest day for me in all of this," Sherry said, "harder than my surgery or my treatments, was the day I had to call my family and tell them that I had cancer. I spent the entire day on the phone letting them know, saying it over and over again. And at the end of the day, I was physically and emotionally exhausted. I didn't want to have to think about having cancer or ever have to say it out loud again. I hadn't told my best girlfriends yet, and since I wasn't willing to speak of my condition any further, I emailed them."

As Sherry sliced out that fat of her story that was her most difficult to chew, I recalled how I, too, became choked by the words of my cancer diagnosis phoning my extended family. I felt like after the sentence had left my mouth, I had been talking about someone else, someone very distant from myself.

"Bless your heart," I returned. "I bet that *was* a hard day, Sherry. And with you having kids, I can't even imagine the whirlwind of feelings and anxieties that must have stirred inside you, consuming your thoughts. I think our imaginations definitely tried to write our diagnosis stories when we held the news inside ourselves. But, once the script left our lips, we realized that it wasn't imaginary anymore. Saying it out loud made it real."

"Man, that's true. And, you know, I say 'yes' to everything now," Sherry remarked. "I stopped saying 'no' because I don't want to miss out on anything." And there it was—a new motto for us all to live by!

"The one thing, though, that I could control in all of this," Sherry continued, "was my attitude. I could sit around and feel sorry for myself, or I could be positive and decide I'm going to kick this. I chose the latter!" she said, proudly.

I would be remiss if I didn't mention that Sherry's passion, which turned into her peace, and later her exercise, was horseback riding. A commonality that she discovered early on that she and Dr. Salydar shared was steeple chasing.

"I think Dr. Salydar books extra time at my appointments with her, because we both know that we're going to need a few minutes to talk about steeple chasing before we move on to my exam," Sherry said, laughing.

I admired Sherry on many levels, as other arenas of life had collided with her cancer, and her fighting aurora had prevailed and withstood it all. She was an inspiration and illustration of where positive thinking and attitude can take you. And it had taken her to lofty places that she had climbed very hard to reach.

Tamara's story:

When I first saw Tamara, she was standing looking out the lodge window sipping coffee. I thought she was shy when I approached her to introduce myself, but as we began chatting, it turned out that she was carrying a cross with more than just her cancer story wrapped around it. She had lost her husband to a brain disease on the 23rd of December, just four months ago, and her cup and heart were full of unresolvedness that still surrounded that loss.

Tamara's home, that sat on forty-five acres, was for sale. "It wasn't home anymore," she said, toughness peering through her tears.

I don't think Tamara realized the strength she had inside as early as the rest of us saw it in her.

"My husband and I were married for twelve years," Tamara went on, "and in that time, I had breast cancer, underwent chemo, and after all of that, my husband was diagnosed with a brain disease that had called me to be a caregiver to him 24/7 for eighteen months. And, there's nothing else I would rather have done than been with him and care for him every minute. He was with me and cared for me every minute of my cancer. It was my turn."

More of the women had now joined our conversation as Tamara continued to share. And, this was the crux of her story that stood out above all else: The deep and genuine love that Tamara had for her husband was apparent like a badge of honor you wear on your sleeve. Her love for him was visibly stamped on her heart, and always would be. It was as if she lived for them both now. Her love for him would always keep him alive inside her, giving her peace and joy for every day. And, this was a peace and joy she freely gave to others, as she reached out with her own courage to reassure and talk with everyone about 'the platters of stale food that life offers up sometimes.'

Tamara's take and attitude on cancer was one that I'd never heard before, and one that I completely loved. She told us, "When I had cancer, people would come up and say to me, 'Aw, I'm sorry you're sick.' I would tell them that I'm not sick. I'm injured. When you're sick, you may not get better. But when you're injured, you always heal."

Through Tamara's earlier dismay, she had instantly lifted us all to newer heights with her fresh perception of cancer. It was truly gift-giving!

Tamara's incredible spirit compelled and reminded each of us to always give our best to life.

Lauren's story:

Lauren was diagnosed in 2012 with breast cancer, and she was a strong, survived veteran of this disease. She had had a bilateral mastectomy with reconstruction and 'all the bells and whistles' of radiation and chemotherapy treatments. She told us that she would have chosen chemo over radiation any day.

"It was so hard to go in, voluntarily, for radiation knowing how bad it was to put into your body. Knowing that radiation, itself, causes cancer and could cause it to return," Lauren proclaimed.

I had never heard anyone say that they would choose chemo over radiation before. Though, I had always heard it the other way around. But, after Lauren spoke her sentiments, it was echoed in agreement among the other women around the table that had experienced both treatment types as well.

Lauren shared that her cancer had put her into the role of Jimmy Stewart from the movie, *It's A Wonderful Life*, in that, she conjured how and what people in her life would do if she wasn't around.

"I found out," Lauren said, "who the people were that really loved me. So many stepped up. And, the ones who didn't that I thought would, I discarded."

That broke my heart to think about the ones who were missing out on knowing and spending time with Lauren. Her vigor, sense of humor, and laughter were all so contagious. And, I had come to the conclusion that Lauren's wonderful finesse, coupled with her feistiness, conveyed to cancer quickly that it had met its match messing with her.

With her continued wit, Lauren went on to tell us about some 'medical marijuana' she had taken on her doctor's referral and close watch, as she just simply couldn't take pills. So, this was a medicine alternative. I had heard about medical marijuana being prescribed before for other cancer patients around the globe for various reasons over news broadcasts aired recently. But the way that Lauren gestured and slipped into the spotlight of a night-club comedian as she unveiled her story to us, definitely made it a more entertaining report than any newscast could ever have pulled off!

Lauren was saying, as she pretended to hold a cigarette to her lips, "Just get high. You'll be fine."

This was her advice to future women diagnosed with cancer who also struggled with swallowing pills. I imagined Lauren as a poster spokeswoman for any cause and platform. Her humor and charisma would *reel in* anyone's trust and everyone's admiration.

As our laughter and moist napkins from our tickled tears had settled, Lauren made a profound remark that completely silenced and summoned all our attention.

"It haunts me," Lauren expressed. "I feel haunted by cancer, as I'm sure we all do. And, even though it's been three years," she continued, with her long locks of brunette hair now fully grown back, "I can still feel it standing here on my shoulder, reminding me that it can come back. My day will be going great, and then, when I get into my car at the end of the day, that's when I feel the tapping on my shoulder and in my mind like its saying, 'Remember me?' It just haunts me like that sometimes."

We all concurred that the ghost of cancer enters our minds and daily thoughts whether we invite it in or not. And, as we sat there, our bodies currently freed from cancer, it was still very much a part of us. It had left its battle scars on us all, but we stood proud and victorious in its defeat.

Until Lauren mentioned it, I never thought of cancer having a voice, or a leg to stand on our shoulders; but I could clearly picture it as a cartooned portrayal. And, in the next frame of the cartoon, I envisioned each of us knocking it off our shoulders and driving away as cancer fled in the opposite direction.

So, the impression that Lauren made on us was that we weren't just BUG SLINGER WARRIORS as our hats and shirts from the fishing event indicated. We were cancer slingers, too!

At the conclusion of our fly-fishing weekend, I had given each of the women an autographed copy of a children's book I had written and published back in 2011. Lauren wittingly asked me when I handed her one, "So, did you have to decide if you liked us before you gave us a copy?"

I jestingly responded back, "No, all of you just had to have bigger breasts than me."

Lauren grabbed me and hugged me, laughing as she said, "So, we won!"

I replied, "You're all winners, but I won the best prize—six new sisters!"

Jane's story:

I think Jane was the youngest among us. I supposed that she was in her early-to-mid-thirties, though I never asked or knew for certain. Even with the short and sparse hair atop her precious head, fashioned with a baseball cap, Jane's glowing youth showed through. And, following our yoga class on Sunday morning, I observed her doing vertical stretches on the wall. As Jane stood there with perfect posture, her arm extended straight up above her head, I thought to myself, *what I would give to have that posture! Yep, she's thirty-something.*

When we had sat around Friday's dinner table telling our tales, Jane professed a thought-provoking statement that sparked an awakening in each of us.

"I think it's harder for our caregivers—our husbands and family members—than it is for us as the patient," Jane declared. "And, my husband is the caregiver times two, because he's also taking care of our three-year-old."

Though we had all known how constant and demanding our bodies need for our family's unwavering care for us had been, Jane's verbal acknowledgement of their dedication, love, and endearing commitment to us was a necessary reminder to never forget.

I had initially thought that Jane was introverted, but she was on the contrary, a ball of lightning energy, laughter, and humility.

Like Carol's story, the story of Jane's surgery never fell within my earshot, but she was still undergoing chemotherapy treatments. And, I remember hearing Jane say that she had 'twenty-three rounds to go.'

Jane was extremely active and ready for any and all planned activities offered during our fly-fishing weekend. I continually witnessed her spunk, joy, and endless tenacity.

Our first morning at breakfast, when I bid Jane a 'good morning' and asked her how she slept, she concernedly, yet comically, began telling me about this stink bug that had taken camp with her in her bunk bed.

"I felt something crawling on my neck," Jane commented, "and when I swatted it away, it ended up on my face, where I think it sprayed me! I quickly jumped down from the top bunk and settled into the bottom one that appeared to be stink bugless, but I didn't sleep much after that, being aware of my shared habitat."

"Oh, my golly, and bless your heart! I think all of our cabins are dotted with these unwelcomed guests," I replied, trying hard not to let my smile slip into a fit of laughter at how hilariously Jane had delivered her nighttime tale.

I'm thinking that Jane's biggest battle may be the one she had with that menacing stink bug.

Kaitlyn's story:

Kaitlyn's story was very humbling, yet also elevating in our awareness to her type of cancerous disease.

"My cancer was in my breast, but it wasn't breast cancer," Kaitlyn remarked as she began her story. "I have angiosarcoma—a rare cancer—that can show up anywhere in the body and later resurface somewhere else."

The room was silent as Kaitlyn's words penetrated our ears, our minds, our hearts.

The exchange promise I made to Kaitlyn in return for sharing her story, at her request, was that I would research and raise written awareness about the scarce form of cancer she bears. In my sincere pleasure of keeping that promise to Kaitlyn, the next several paragraphs outline the definition, symptoms, anatomy locations, and treatments of angiosarcoma. While this disease is uncommon, it chose an exceptional woman and force to contend with in Kaitlyn.

Angiosarcoma is best defined as "an uncommon malignant tumor originating in a blood vessel."[1]

"*Hemangiosarcomas* start in blood vessel walls and *lymphangiosarcomas* start in lymph vessel walls. *Angiosarcomas* may occur in any organ of the body but are more frequently found in skin and soft tissue. They can also originate in the liver, breast, spleen, bone, or heart."[2]

"Soft-tissue sarcomas are a family of cancers that arise from supportive (connective) tissue other than the bones. Specifically, soft-tissue sarcomas may afflict the muscles, fibrous tissue, fat cells, the blood vessels (angiosarcoma), and the joints. Soft-tissue sarcoma usually starts as a painless mass or lump, although in some cases pain occurs before the lump, but only for a short time since these cancers can grow rapidly. Any unexplained lump should be investigated promptly.

In addition to a thorough physical examination, specific diagnostic studies used when soft-tissue sarcoma is suspected include (depending upon the affected part), X-rays, CT scans, ultrasonic (echo) examinations, kidney studies and others. A biopsy is an essential diagnostic step, and precautions such as those followed for bone biopsies should be taken. Tissue for biopsy may be obtained either through a surgical incision or with a hollow needle."[3]

"The cause of *angiosarcomas* is usually unknown. The tumors may develop as a complication of a pre-existing condition. Certain patient groups may be at greater risk of developing *angiosarcomas*. These include the following: 1) patients with chronic lymphoedema (accumulation of lymph fluid in the arms) who have undergone a radical mastectomy for breast cancer (removal of breast and all lymph nodes under the arm); 2) radio-therapy patients; 3) patients with foreign material such as Dacron, shrapnel, steel, and plastic in the body; and, 4) patients exposed to environmental agents such as sprays containing arsenic and vinyl chloride in the plastic industry."[4]

"The signs and symptoms of *angiosarcomas* differ according to the location of the tumor. Often symptoms of the disease are not apparent until the tumor is well advanced.

The characteristic signs of angiosarcoma in the breast are: 1) rapidly enlarging palpable mass without tenderness; 2) often there is no pain; and, 3) tumors often grow deep within breast tissue and cause diffuse breast enlargement with associated bluish skin discoloration."[5]

"Before developing a treatment plan, staging to determine the extent of disease, specific type of cancer, as well as the tumor's location, is usually recommended. Microscopic examination of the sarcoma cells also is recommended by many authorities to determine the cell grade.

The treatment of soft-tissue sarcoma has traditionally involved extensive surgery aimed at removing the cancer and surrounding tissue. Often this meant limb amputation and removal of muscles. More recently, however, a combination of treatments—less radical surgery, radiation therapy, and chemotherapy—has been used with good results. The timing and administration of the treatments depends upon staging, grade and other circumstances. In most cases limbs and muscles can be saved without lowering the rate of cure. Surgical treatment, however, may entail removal of the lymph nodes from the area of the tumor to help prevent the cancer's spread to other parts of the body. Post-surgery radiation therapy may be given to the tumor site and regional lymph nodes. The prognosis for soft-tissue sarcoma appears to be improving with the increased use of combination treatment."[6]

The treatments that Kaitlyn had undergone thus far included radiation, chemotherapy, and visits to Johns Hopkins in collaboration and cooperation with her Martha Jefferson team of doctors.

Kaitlyn's precious curls framed her face and tears overtook her words for just a moment as she said, "My prognosis could be grim, and in a year or so, it could be curtains for me. But I'm going to live my life, because I'm alive and well, now."

I sat there wondering, *what's another word for huge inspiration?!*

I don't believe that it's going to be 'curtains' anytime soon for Kaitlyn. On the contrary, I think her debut in life is just beginning. And, here's the proof: Kaitlyn was the big catcher on the lake that weekend, hooking and reeling in 3+ fish her first day out. And, on Sunday, Kaitlyn got up close and personal with the fish as she entered their watery home in full-body waders. Watch out fish! Watch out angiosarcoma!!

We were all detoured, but the road we ended up on was better and more solid than the one that we traveled before it. Because God carried us, led us, and drove us safely thru this unfamiliar byway, revealing to us that some of life's greatest blessings are found in detours.

Our journeys through cancer brought us to this place—this fly-fishing retreat—so that we could be part of a sisterhood grander than any we could ever have imagined, wearing armor of courage and strength larger than we ever knew we had.

And I realized something bigger than myself surrounded among this humble fellowship of incredible women: the sigh of relief, the abiding hope, and the joyful celebration that comes with battling and surviving cancer. And, the marvelous therapy found in high peaks and running waters spun around a threaded fishing pole that brings a whole new *catch* to healing!

We are the Bug Slinger Warriors.

ACKNOWLEDGMENTS

MY SINCERE AND heartfelt thanks to my unsurpassed and Heaven-sent team of physicians and supporting staff at Martha Jefferson Hospital for their unwavering dedication, level of care, and medical expertise in the fight against cancer. While their names in this book are fictitious to protect their privacy, their contributions to the advancements of cancer care and treatment options are very real.

I am deeply grateful to my family and friends whose words of encouragement, countless kind gestures, and steadfast prayers made unimaginable days, reimagined.

An unforgettable thanks to my best friend and sister, Vickie, who comfortably stays seated during a crisis, but for me, stood tall and remained standing.

A there-are-not-enough-words thanks to my Godsent and amazing husband whose name really is John and whose character really is as described and told about in this story. He is the fabric of the best of everything in my life. And John is also an outstanding assistant in slaying an octopus!

I express unending gratitude to my warrior sisters of the 2015 Spring Fly Fling Fly-Fishing Retreat for allowing me to 'tie' their beautiful stories of strength and tenacity into the fibers of this book. I feel so blessed that our varying paths led us to the same running river where our sisterhood flowed and trickles on. I will continue to be inspired and in awe of every one of them every single day! Though the names of these remarkable bug and cancer slinger women have been changed for privacy purposes, their experiences remain real, and their blessings identifiable. And, a special thanks to Mark Andrews, the extraordinary founder of Therapeutic Adventures, Inc. for making the meeting of the poles possible!

To my God, Lord of my life, I offer my infinite gratefulness for Your merciful healing within every facet of me. For the marathon training at my workplace so I could walk; for Your whisper replies whether I had a question or not; for Your calm reassurances when I was so unsure; for the fear You bore for me when things were unbearable; for Your constant relief in the midst of pain; for meeting me in the scary places where You were the only escape; and, for every impossible turn, every steep hill, every dark tunnel, every impassible path, and every detour that You held the keys and drove me through because I didn't know the way; and the only way was You! I eternally thank You.

And, thank you, dear reader. May you find comfort in knowing that God is by your side in every step you take. And even far ahead of you to keep you safe. He is always listening and waiting for you to call upon Him. Whether chauffeur, pilot, or trail guide, God has delivered countless people out of the darkest forests while wearing all sorts of hats!

ENDNOTES

1. Arthur I. Holleb, M.D., "Glossary," in *The American Cancer Society Cancer Book,* (New York: Doubleday & Company, Inc., 1986), 624.

2. Karen Bellenir, *Cancer Sourcebook, Health Reference Series,* 5th ed., (Michigan: Omnigraphics, Inc., 2007), 798.

3. Norman Jaffe, M.D., "Cancer of the Bone and Connective Tissue," in *The American Cancer Society Cancer Book,* (New York: Doubleday & Company, Inc., 1986), 274.

4. Bellenir, *Cancer Sourcebook,* 798.

5. Ibid, 799.

6. Jaffe, *The American Cancer Society,* 275.